KNIT yOUR Own ZOMBIE

FIONA GOBLE

KNIT YOUR OWN ZOMBIE

Over **1,000** COMBINATIONS
to RIP'N'REASSEMBLE
for HORRIFYING RESULTS

Adamsmedia

Published by
Adams Media, a division of F+W Media, Inc.
57 Littlefield Street, Avon, MA 02322. U.S.A.
www.adamsmedia.com

ISBN-10: 1-4405-5716-0
ISBN-13: 978-1-4405-5716-3
eISBN-10: 1-4405-5717-9
eISBN-13: 978-1-4405-5717-0

Printed in China

Color origination by Ivy Press Reprographics

10 9 8 7 6 5 4 3 2 1

Library of Congress Cataloging-in-Publication Data is available from the publisher.

This book was conceived, designed, and produced by

Ivy Press
Creative Director Peter Bridgewater
Publisher Susan Kelly
Commissioning Editor Sophie Collins
Editorial Director Tom Kitch
Art Director James Lawrence
Designer Clare Barber
Photographer Andrew Perris

Important safety information
Many of the knitted figures are small or have removable parts, making them a choking hazard. They are not suitable for children under the age of 36 months.

CONTENTS

THE ZOMBIES

INTRODUCTION

When knits go wrong, things can turn very bad indeed. This book offers you nine monstrous zombie characters, each with his or her own unique accoutrements, and all chillingly simple to knit. And there's something even better: Every part of every zombie is rip 'n' grip—heads and limbs are attached to the body using Velcro, so you can tear them apart like a toddler having a tantrum, then reassemble them in any way you want to create brand-new creations that are unique to you.

You'll find that ripping the head off one of these little monsters is strangely therapeutic—once a knitted zombie has taken up residence on your desk, those tiresome executive toys will be a thing of the past. You can dispense with that rubbery stress ball or the boring book on mindfulness meditation. Just tear up a zombie for an immediate lift.

There's a veritable smorgasbord of choices, too. From Zombie Cop to Frankenstein's Monster, each of the nine characters has his or her own outfit, accessories—and body parts. Start with Classic Zombie—he (or is it she?) is simple enough. Then make a pair, or three, or four . . . Mix and match their accessories as well as their limbs and heads. See how Zombie Grave Digger looks holding her own skull under her arm, but wearing someone else's head. However you mix them, there will always be other enticing combinations you can try.

Your WORKBOX

You only need some basic tools and materials to get started on your terrifying knitted zombies. However, it's a good idea to check through your workbox before you begin to make sure that you have got everything you need.

KNITTING NEEDLES

The projects in this book are knitted using a pair of size U.S. 2/3 (3 mm) standard knitting needles. If size U.S. 2.5 knitting needles are available to you, that is ideal. If not, both size U.S. 2 or size U.S. 3 will work. To complete some projects, you will need a pair of size U.S. 2 (2.75 mm) knitting needles, too. The needles for each project are listed in the individual sections.

CROCHET HOOK

While the patterns do not involve actual crocheting, a crochet hook in size U.S. D-3 (3.25 mm) is needed to create crochet chains used for some details. Instructions are given within the patterns. If you already have a similar crochet hook but not in the identical size, it will be okay.

YARN NEEDLE

You will need a sewing needle with a large eye and a blunt end (sometimes called a yarn needle) to sew your work together. A tapestry needle will work too.

EMBROIDERY NEEDLE

You will need an embroidery needle with an eye large enough to thread a length of DK yarn for embroidering the zombies' details. These needles have more pointed ends than tapestry needles, allowing you to get between the strands of your yarn, which is crucial for working some stitches.

STANDARD SEWING NEEDLE

You will need an ordinary sewing needle to sew on the fastenings and some of the decorations, such as buttons and beads.

WATER-SOLUBLE PEN

This is useful to mark the position of the dolls' features and markings before you sew them. Water-soluble pens are like ordinary felt pens, but the ink disappears when sprayed or dabbed with water. The ink is safe to use on almost all yarns and fabrics, but it is worth testing beforehand to make sure.

STITCH HOLDER

This gadget is useful to hold extra stitches while you are working on a separate part of your knitting. You could also use an extra needle or large safety pins instead, because the projects are so small.

PENCIL

You will need one to draw around the templates to create some of the zombies' accessories—an ordinary pencil is fine.

GREEN AND GRAY CRAYONS

These are useful for coloring in some of the zombies' flesh—particularly around the eyes.

SMALL SCISSORS

A pair of small, sharp scissors is vital for trimming yarn tails without the risk of cutting your knitting.

HOUSEHOLD SCISSORS

You will need these to cut out your card-stock templates for a few of the zombie accessories.

JEWELER'S PLIERS

This tool will be useful to add the jump rings to any charms you use and to create the handcuffs for the Zombie Cop.

TAPE MEASURE

You will need one to check the positioning of some of the fastenings and for measuring the length of your crochet chains. You may also need it to measure your yarns.

Yarns and Other StUFF YoU NEED

To make the projects in this book, you will need a selection of standard DK (double knitting) yarn. To make some of the clothes, hair, and accessories, you will also need some special types of yarn. These and a few other essential materials are all mentioned here.

YARNS

The main parts of all the projects in the book are knitted in standard DK yarns. We recommend that you use 100 percent wool yarns or ones that contain at least 20 percent wool. Yarns made from 100 percent acrylic or 100 percent cotton do not have the natural stretch of wool-base yarns and the results can be disappointing.

For some of the clothes, you will also need some special-effect DK yarn. For other items, you will need sock yarn or 4-ply yarn, both of which are thinner than DK yarn and widely available. Some of the hair is created using mohair yarn or a yarn made from a mixture of mohair and silk, which is a light, fluffy yarn and ideal for recreating wispy, zombielike hair. For a few of the accessories, you will also need small amounts of dark silver metallic crochet yarn. All the yarns are listed in the "You will need" section for the individual projects and can be bought from your local knitting supplier.

STANDARD SEWING THREAD

You will need thread to sew the fastenings to your projects and to sew on the buttons and beads. You do not need a variety of colors—all the projects in the book use only cream sewing thread.

POLYESTER TOY FILLING

This is a soft, fluffy filling made from 100 percent polyester that is specially made to stuff toys and handcrafted items. It is widely available in craft stores. Make sure that the one you choose conforms to all relevant safety standards.

FASTENING TAPE

The main zombie body parts are joined together with Velcro "hook-and-loop" tape, so you can dismember your doll and mix and match components from different zombie dolls. Make sure you buy the sew-in version of the tape (not the self-adhesive or iron-on versions) and choose a color that most closely matches your doll. The tape is normally available in white and black, but you can also buy it in beige in some craft stores.

SNAP FASTENERS

Each zombie's arms are joined to the body using ½-inch (13-mm) snap fasteners. Buy these from a store that sells sewing accessories.

BUTTONS AND BEADS

To create some of the zombies' teeth, fingernails, and accessories, you will need a few buttons, beads, bows, and other items. Before you buy something specially for a project, first search through your workbox to see what else could be used. You do not need to use the exact items that we show in the project—sometimes you can discover a great look when you are least expecting it by experimenting.

PLASTIC DRINKING STRAWS

These are used to create some of the zombie accessories.

CARD STOCK

You will need a small amount of silver or gray card stock to make templates for some accessories.

CHARMS

A few of the zombies have special jewelry created from spooky metal charms. These are available in some craft and bead stores or from online suppliers.

A FEW EXTRAS

One or two of the projects require some less usual but still widely available items, such as metal rings, waxed cord, and lengths of jewelry-making chain. See the "You will need" section in the individual projects to discover what you need for each zombie.

GAUGE

The knitting gauge for the patterns in this book is 12 sts and 16 rows to 1½ inches (4 cm) square over st st on U.S. 2/3 (3 mm) needles.

The gauge when knitting small items, such as the ones in this book, is not normally as crucial as when you are knitting clothes. The main concern is to make sure that your knitting is firm, so that your items keep their shape and the stuffing does not show through the knitted fabric. However, if you knit unusually tightly, you may want to use slightly larger needles than recommended. If you knit loosely, you may want to choose slightly smaller knitting needles.

AbBReVIATiONS

You will find the following knitting abbreviations in this book.

( )	number in parentheses refers to how many stitches should be on your needle
[ ]	repeat the directions within the square brackets the number of times indicated
*	marks the start and end of a section of the knitting pattern to be repeated later when instructed
K	knit
P	purl
st(s)	stitch(es)
st st	stockinette stitch
beg	beginning
k2tog	knit the next 2 stitches together
p2tog	purl the next 2 stitches together
kwise	by knitting the stitch or stitches
pwise	by purling the stitch or stitches
inc1	increase one stitch by knitting into the front and then the back of the next stitch
M1	make one stitch by picking up the horizontal loop before the next stitch and knitting into the back of it.
s1	slip one (slip a stitch onto the right-hand needle without knitting it)
psso	pass slipped stitch over (pass the slipped stitch over the stitch just knitted)
ssk	slip, slip, knit (slip two stitches, one at a time, then knit together the slipped stitches)
RS	right side
WS	wrong side
yo	yarn over (bring your yarn over from the back to the front of your work)
cont	continue
rem	remaining
rep	repeat
oz	ounce
g	gram
in	inch
mm	millimeter
cm	centimeter
yd	yard
m	meter

The Guts OF THE MATTER

All knitting is made up from two basic stitches—the knit stitch and the purl stitch. You'll also need to know how to cast on and bind off. If you want to refresh your memory for knitting basics before you begin, you're in the right place. For a few of the projects, you'll need to know a couple of intermediate techniques: eyelet knitting and knitting with two colors at once.

CASTING ON

1 Make a slip knot by making a simple loop of yarn and pulling another loop of yarn through it. Insert your needle through the loop and pull the slip knot up firmly. This is your first cast-on stitch.

2 To make the next cast-on stitch, hold the needle with the slip knot in your left hand. Insert the point of your right-hand needle through the slip knot from left to right. Wind your yarn around the needle tip.

3 Use the tip of your needle to pull a loop of yarn through the first cast-on stitch. You now have your second cast-on stitch.

4 Transfer the new stitch to the left-hand needle.

5 To make your third cast-on stitch, insert your right-hand needle between the two stitches on the left-hand needle. Then wind your yarn around the needle, as shown in step 2.

6 Use the tip of your needle to pull a loop of yarn through the gap between the stitches, and then transfer this new stitch to your left-hand needle.

Repeat the last two steps until you have the number of stitches you need.

KNITTING

1 Insert your right-hand needle from left to right into the front of the first stitch to be knitted.

2 Wind your yarn around the needle from left to right.

3 Use the tip of your needle to draw a loop of yarn through the stitch. This is your new stitch.

4 Pull your right-hand needle gently to the right, so that the original stitch comes off the left-hand needle.

Repeat these steps until you have knitted all your stitches. To get ready for the next row, put the needle with all the stitches into your left hand.

PURLING

This is like making a knit stitch in reverse.

1 With your yarn at the front of your work, insert your right-hand needle from right to left into the front of the first stitch that is on your left-hand needle.

2 Wind your yarn around the tip of your needle from top to bottom.

3 Use the tip of your needle to pull a loop of yarn through the original stitch. This is your new stitch.

4 Pull your right-hand needle gently to the right, so that the original stitch comes off the left-hand needle.

Repeat these steps until you have purled all the stitches on the left-hand needle. To get ready for the next row, put the needle with all the stitches into your left hand.

BIND OFF KNITWISE

1 Knit two stitches in the normal way. With the tip of your left-hand needle, lift the first stitch you have knitted over the second knitted stitch.

2 Knit the next stitch so that there are two stitches on your needle again, and repeat step 1.

Continue in this way until you have just one stitch left. Trim the yarn, leaving a long enough tail that you can use for sewing your item together, and then pull your last stitch through.

BIND OFF PURLWISE

This is just like binding off knitwise, but you purl the stitches instead of knitting them.

1 Purl two stitches in the normal way. With the tip of your left-hand needle, lift the first stitch you have purled over the second purled stitch.

2 Purl the next stitch so that you have two stitches on your needle again, and repeat step 1.

Continue in this way until you have just one stitch left. Trim the yarn, leaving a long enough tail that you can use for sewing together your item, and then pull your last stitch through.

COMBINING KNIT AND PURL STITCHES

When you knit every row, the knitted fabric that you produce is called garter stitch.

When you work alternate rows of knit and purl stitches, the knitted fabric that you produce is called stocking or stockinette stitch, which is the main stitch used for the projects in this book.

When you work vertical rows of knit and purl stitches by combining the two stitches in one row, the knitted fabric that you produce is called ribbing or rib stitch.

EYELET KNITTING

This is created by working a combination of knit and purl stitches and a special stitch that involves taking your yarn from the back to the front of your work (written in the patterns as yo or yarn over) and then knitting together two stitches. The loop that is created from taking your yarn to the front of your work creates an additional stitch.

KNITTING WITH TWO COLORS

This is just like ordinary knitting, but you work some stitches in one color and others in a second color. The most important thing to remember is to carry the color you are not using loosely across the back of your work. If you pull it too tightly, your knitting will pucker and look misshapen.

Shape SHiFTiNG

To create your zombies, you will need to feel confident about shaping your work using a variety of methods to increase and decrease the number of stitches on your needle. Read on to discover more.

INCREASING M1

The main way to increase the number of stitches on your needle is to make an additional stitch between two stitches. This is written as M1—or "make 1" stitch.

1 Use the tip of your right-hand needle to pick up the horizontal loop between the stitch you have just knitted and the following stitch.

2 Transfer the loop onto your left-hand needle by inserting the needle into the front of the loop. Then you can knit into the back of the loop in the normal way.

3 Your new stitch will now be on your right-hand needle.

INCREASING INC1

In some cases, you will need to increase the number of stitches slightly differently.

Begin by knitting your stitch in the normal way, but instead of slipping the original stitch off the needle, knit again into the back of the original stitch. Now you can slip the original stitch off the needle.

DECREASING K2TOG

This is the simplest way of decreasing a stitch and involves putting your needle through two stitches instead of one, then knitting them in the normal way.

DECREASING P2TOG

This is just like knitting two stitches together, only you purl the stitches instead of knitting them.

DECREASING SSK

This forms a mirror image to the right-sloping stitch formed by knitting two stitches together. First slip one stitch, then the next stitch, from your left-hand needle to your right-hand needle. Insert the tip of your left-hand needle from left to right through the front of the two slipped stitches, then knit them in the normal way.

DECREASING S1, K2TOG, PSSO

Occasionally you will need to decrease two stitches at a time. For this, first slip one stitch from your left- to your right-hand needle. Then knit two stitches together, as outlined above. Now pass the slipped stitch over the stitch you have just made.

Joining

It can often seem that joining your knitted pieces together takes longer than the knitting itself. However, it really is important to take your time during this stage to make sure that you are happy with your finished items.

MATTRESS STITCH

This stitch is used to seam vertical edges, such as the side seams of bodies and garments. A slight variation of the stitch is used to join two horizontal edges, such as the lower edges of the zombie bodies.

VERTICAL EDGES

With the two vertical edges together, take your yarn under the running stitch between the first two stitches on one side, then under the running stitch between the first two stitches on the other side. Continue threading your yarn up the seam in this way, pulling the yarn up firmly every few stitches.

HORIZONTAL EDGES

With the two horizontal edges together, take your yarn around the two "legs" of the outermost row of stitches on one piece of knitting and then under the two corresponding "legs" of the second piece of knitting. Continue in this way, pulling the yarn up firmly every few stitches.

WHIPSTITCHING

This is used for joining curved edges or sewing small items together. For most projects, you will use a combination of whipstitch and mattress stitch. The stitch is usually worked on the reverse side of your knitting but is sometimes used on the front.

To whipstitch a seam, take your yarn from the front over the edges of your seam and back through the front, a little farther along.

PICKING UP STITCHES ALONG A HORIZONTAL EDGE

Sometimes you will need to pick up stitches along a horizontal edge of your knitting in order to knit another part of the project.

With the right side of your work facing you, insert your needle into the first stitch where you want to create a new stitch. Wind the yarn around the tip of your needle and pull the new loop through, just as if you were knitting a normal stitch. Continue until you have the required number of stitches.

The Finishing Line

To add finishing touches, such as blood splats, wounds, and gruesome facial features, to your knitted items, you will need to know a few basic embroidery stitches and some other useful techniques and handy hints.

FRENCH KNOT

This is used for the centers of some of the eyes and for the blood splats and pimples.

Bring your yarn out at your starting point, within the yarn strand instead of between stitches. Wind the yarn twice around your needle, keeping the yarn somewhat taut. Take the point of your needle back down into your knitting, just by your starting point, again within the yarn strand. Bring your needle out at the starting point for the next stitch or in an inconspicuous area where you can secure and trim the yarn. Pull your yarn through your work so that the knot slides off the needle and onto your knitting.

CHAIN STITCH

This is used for the eyes, some of the noses, wounds, edging for holes, and other markings. You can work chain stitch in rows, curved lines, or circles.

Bring your yarn out at your starting point. Take your needle back into your knitting, just by your starting point, leaving a small loop of yarn. Bring your needle back up through your knitting a stitch's width along and catch the yarn loop. Pull your yarn up somewhat firmly. Repeat this process until the stitching is the required length.

STRAIGHT STITCH

This is used for the stitches worked over the wounds and scars and for a few other decorative touches. Simply take your yarn out at your starting point and back down into your knitting where you want the stitch to end. Bring your needle back out at the point where you want to make the next stitch.

SATIN STITCH

This stitch is used for some of the zombies' mouths. It consists of a series of straight stitches worked closely together.

Take your needle out at your starting point. Insert your needle back into your work and out again near the starting point, ready to make the next stitch. Continue in this way until the shape is filled.

USING A SEPARATED STRAND

For some of the embroidery, you will need to separate your yarn into two thinner lengths or—in a few cases—into a single strand. Separated strands can be delicate. To make sure your yarn doesn't break, always pull on it gently from close to your work. You should also make sure that the length of yarn you are working with is no longer than you need.

STARTING AND FINISHING EMBROIDERY

To begin embroidering on your zombies, tie a double knot in the end of your yarn. Position your needle between stitches at the back of your work (or a nearby inconspicuous area) and bring it out to your starting point. Pull gently on the yarn so that the knot disappears into the inside of your work. When you have finished the embroidery, bring your yarn back out to an inconspicuous area. Work a couple of tiny stitches, one over the other, around the running thread between the knitted stitches. (The running threads will be slightly sunken so the stitches will be virtually invisible.) Conceal the remaining yarn tail as outlined under Weaving In Ends (see right).

When you are working embroidery on a flat item, such as the zombies' clothes, you can simply tie a knot in your yarn at both the beginning and end of your work, and trim the yarn closely.

CROCHET CHAINS

1 Form a slip knot on your crochet hook, as if you were starting to cast on some knitting. Wind the yarn around your crochet hook from the back to the front, catching the yarn in the slot of the hook.

2 Use the hook to pull a loop of yarn through the slip stitch to form the second chain. Continue in this way, pulling each loop up tightly, until your chain is the required length.

SOAK AWAY

Sometimes when you have sewn an item together, the shape is not exactly as you want. In this case, soak the item in lukewarm water, then squeeze out the excess water, reshape the item, and let it dry.

SEWING ON FASTENINGS

Sew the Velcro tape to your knitting by whipstitching around the edges. Remember to take your needle fairly deeply into your work to make sure the tape is secure.

Sew the snap fasteners to your knitting by sewing several times through the four holes on the outside edge of the fasteners. It is helpful to double up your thread when you do this to make it stronger. Take your needle fairly deeply into your work to make sure the fasteners are secure and remember not to pull too tightly or you will risk breaking the thread on the edges of the hole.

SEWING ON BUTTONS AND BEADS

Secure the buttons using normal sewing thread. Secure the beads by working a few backstitches through the hole in each bead, again using normal sewing thread.

WEAVING IN ENDS

You can conceal the yarn ends, or "tails," on stuffed items within the item itself. Use your needle to take the yarn end into the item and out again. Squash the item slightly, pull the yarn taut, and then trim it close to your knitting. When the item regains its normal shape, the yarn end will be concealed inside.

With certain items, such as the zombies' clothes, weave in the yarn tails by working a few running stitches back and forth along the seam allowance. It helps to work the running stitches within the yarn strands so they stay put.

ReanimAting YOUR ZoMbIES

All the zombies in this book are constructed using the same general sewing techniques. The Velcro and snap fasteners allow you to rip them up with ease!

THE HEAD

Place the two head pieces right sides together and whipstitch around the sides and lower edge of the head. Turn the piece right side out. Stuff and then close the top of the head, using mattress stitch. Sew the loop part of the Velcro fastening to the center back of the head. The fastening should be vertical and the lower edge should be about ¾ inch (1.5 cm) up from the bottom of the head.

THE UPPER BODY

Form the front upper body piece into a box shape, so that the right side of your knitting is on the inside of the "box." Whipstitch the short seams at the corners. Turn the "box" right side out. Join the back upper body piece to the front using mattress stitch, leaving the lower edge open for stuffing. Stuff the piece and close the lower edge, using mattress stitch.

THE LOWER BODY AND LEGS

Join the front and back of the lower body in the same way as the upper body.

Attach the hook part of the Velcro fastening to the top of the lower body and the loop part to the lower part of the upper body.

Fold the leg pieces in half lengthwise so that the right sides are together. Whipstitch the lower, back, and top seams of the foot. Turn the piece right side out and use mattress stitch to sew the back leg seams. Stuff the legs and whipstitch them to the bottom of the lower body.

ARMS

Fold the arm pieces in half lengthwise, so that the right side of your knitting is on the inside. Whipstitch around the hand. Turn the piece right side out and use mattress stitch to sew the arm seams. Stuff lightly. Fold the top flap of the arm down across the opening to form a flat surface and whipstitch the edges in place. Sew the stud side of the snap fasteners to the flat top section of each arm. Sew the socket side of the snap fasteners to the top sides of the upper body.

Classic ZOMBIE

People (that's you, dear reader) are used to zombies. They've featured in our movies for decades now, in all kinds of forms, from the silent, somewhat dignified early option—check out *I Walked With a Zombie* (1943)—to the much more aggressive creations of George Romero or Quentin Tarantino. To start you off on your knitting journey, we're opening with Classic Zombie. Disheveled and damaged, yet disconcertingly lively, his vibe is energetic, even upbeat—this is one zombie who's ready to rumble.

THEY WON'T STAY DEAD!

An IMAGE TEN Production

NIGHT OF THE LIVING DEAD

They keep coming back in a bloodthirsty lust for HUMAN FLESH!...

Pits the dead against the living in a struggle for survival!

Starring JUDITH O'DEA · DUANE JONES · MARILYN EASTMAN · KARL HARDMAN · JUDITH RIDLEY · KEITH WAYNE

PEDIGREE

1929 *The Magic Island*, the first novel introducing the word "zombie" to popular culture, is published.

1936 Boris Karloff stars in *The Walking Dead*; more than 70 years later, a smash-hit U.S. television series of the same name prompted a fresh zombie craze.

1968 The introduction of recognizable zombies in the modern style, with the release of George Romero's *Night of the Living Dead* (left).

Classic ZOMBIE

With his dangling eye and gaping mouth, this apparition is every inch the classic zombie. Dressed in dowdy, tattered clothes and with the last word in bad hair days, this poor guy has wounds all over the place, and his guts are spilling out of his middle in vile woolly festoons. However, don't worry too much—they tuck neatly into their own specially made pouch should you prefer it that way.

YOU WILL NEED

1 skein beige DK yarn; 225 yd (206 m) per 3.5 oz (100 g)

Small amounts of dark red, cream, and dark gray DK yarns

1 skein bright red DK yarn; 225 yd (206 m) per 3.5 oz (100 g)

Very small amounts of purple and black DK yarns

Small amount of yellow mohair or mohair/silk yarn

1 skein rust 4-ply yarn; 494 yd (452 m) per 3.5 oz (100 g)

1 skein variegated gray 4-ply yarn; 494 yd (452 m) per 3.5 oz (100 g)

1 oz/30 g polyester toy filling

Cream sewing thread

Twelve medium dark green bugle beads

Three small white bugle beads

A glass bead for the eye

A piece of Velcro tape in white, measuring 1 x ³⁄₈ in (2.5 x 1 cm)

A piece of Velcro tape in white, measuring 2 x ³⁄₄ in (5 x 2 cm)

Two ¹⁄₂-in (13-mm) snap fasteners

YOU WILL ALSO NEED

A pair of U.S. 2/3 (3 mm) knitting needles

A yarn needle to sew your items together

An embroidery needle

An ordinary sewing needle

A gray crayon

THE DOLL

HEAD

MAKE 2 PIECES

- Cast on 10 sts in beige.
- Work 6 rows in st st, beg with a K row.
- Next row: [K1, M1] twice, K6, [M1, K1] twice. (14 sts)
- Next row: P.
- Next row: K2, M1, K to last 2 sts, M1, K2. (16 sts)
- Next row: P.
- Rep last 2 rows 1 more time. (18 sts)
- Work 12 rows in st st, beg with a K row.
- Next row: K2, [k2tog] twice, K6, [ssk] twice, K2. (14 sts)
- Next row: P2tog, P10, p2tog. (12 sts)
- Bind off.

UPPER BODY

The upper body is knitted from the top to the bottom.

FRONT

MAKE 1

- Cast on 14 sts in beige.
- Work 6 rows in st st, beg with a K row.
- Next row: Cast on 4 sts, K to end. (18 sts)
- Next row: Cast on 4 sts, P to end. (22 sts)
- Work 10 rows in st st, beg with a K row.
- Next row: K8, P3, then turn and work on only these 11 sts, leaving rem 11 sts on needle.
- Next row: K3, P8.
- Next row: K8, P3.
- Rep last 2 rows 4 more times.
- Break yarn and join it to rem 11 sts on RS of work.
- Next row: P3, K8.
- Next row: P8, K3.
- Rep last 2 rows 4 more times.
- Next row: P3, K8.

- Now work across all 22 sts.
- Work 2 rows in st st, beg with a P row.
- Next row: P4, K14, P4.
- Next row: Bind off 4 sts, K to last 4 sts, bind off 4 sts. (14 sts)
- Break yarn and rejoin it to WS of work.
- Work 5 rows in st st, beg with a P row.
- Bind off.

BACK

MAKE 1

- Cast on 14 sts in beige.
- Work 24 rows in st st, beg with a K row.
- Bind off.

GUT POCKET

MAKE 1

- Cast on 8 sts in beige.
- 1st row: Inc1, K to last 2 sts, inc1, K1. (10 sts)
- Next row: P.
- Rep last 2 rows 1 more time. (12 sts)
- Work 10 rows in st st, beg with a K row.
- Next row: K1, k2tog, K to last 3 sts, ssk, K1. (10 sts)
- Next row: P.
- Rep last 2 rows 1 more time. (8 sts)
- Bind off.

GUTS

STOMACH

MAKE 1

- Cast on 5 sts in dark red.
- 1st row: Inc1, K2, inc1, K1. (7 sts)
- Next row: P.
- Next row: K1, M1, K to last st, M1, K1. (9 sts)
- Next row: P.
- Rep last 2 rows 1 more time. (11 sts)

- Work 4 rows in st st, beg with a K row.
- Next row: K1, k2tog, K to last 3 sts, ssk, K1. (9 sts)
- Next row: P.
- Rep last 2 rows 1 more time. (7 sts)
- Next row: K1, k2tog, K1, ssk, K1. (5 sts)
- Bind off kwise.

INTESTINES

MAKE 1

- Cast on 40 sts in dark red.
- 1st row: K.
- Bind off.

LOWER BODY
FRONT
MAKE 1
- Cast on 14 sts in beige.
- Work 6 rows in st st, beg with a K row.
- Next row: Cast on 4 sts, K to end. (18 sts)
- Next row: Cast on 4 sts, P to end. (22 sts)
- Work 7 rows in st st, beg with a K row.
- Next row: P4, K14, P4.
- Next row: Bind off 4 sts, K to last 4 sts, bind off 4 sts. (14 sts)
- Break yarn and rejoin it to WS of work.
- Work 5 rows in st st, beg with a P row.
- Bind off.

BACK
MAKE 1
- Cast on 14 sts in beige.
- Work 8 rows in st st, beg with a K row.
- Bind off.

FIRST LEG
MAKE 1
- Cast on 30 sts in beige.
- Work 6 rows in st st, beg with a K row.
- Next row: K6, bind off 18 sts, K to end. (12 sts) *
- Work 23 rows in st st, beg with a P row.
- Bind off.

SECOND LEG
OUTER LEG
MAKE 1
- Work as for first leg until *.
- Work 5 rows in st st, beg with a P row.
- Next row: K5, P2, then turn and work on only these 7 sts, leaving rem 5 sts on needle.
- Next row: K2, P5.
- Next row: K5, P2.
- Rep last 2 rows 5 more times.
- Break yarn and rejoin it to rem 5 sts on RS of work.
- Next row: P2, K3.
- Next row: P3, K2.
- Next row: P2, K3.
- Rep last 2 rows 5 more times.
- Now work across all 12 sts.

- Work 5 rows in st st, beg with a P row.
- Bind off.

INNER LEG
MAKE 1
- Cast on 26 sts in bright red.
- Work 4 rows in st st, beg with a K row.
- Next row: K5, bind off 16 sts, K to end. (10 sts)
- Work 21 rows in st st, beg with a P row.
- Bind off.

FIRST ARM
MAKE 1
- Cast on 4 sts in beige.
- Work 4 rows in st st, beg with a K row.
- Next row: Cast on 3 sts, K to end. (7 sts)
- Next row: Cast on 3 sts, P to end. (10 sts) *
- Work 30 rows in st st, beg with a K row.
- Next row: K1, k2tog, K4, ssk, K1. (8 sts)
- Next row: P2tog, P4, p2tog. (6 sts)
- Break yarn, thread it through rem sts, and secure.

SECOND ARM
OUTER ARM
MAKE 1
- Work as for first arm until *.
- Work 20 rows in st st, beg with a K row.
- Break yarn and thread it through rem sts, but do not pull up tightly or secure.

INNER ARM
MAKE 1
- Cast on 8 sts in bright red.
- Work 28 rows in st st, beg with a K row.

- Next row: K1, k2tog, K2, ssk, K1. (6 sts)
- Next row: P2tog, P2, p2tog. (4 sts)
- Break yarn, thread it through rem sts, and secure.

MAKING UP AND DECORATING

To make the split on the elbow of the second arm, embroider a ring of small, tight chain stitches in beige and snip the threads within the circle to create a hole.

Sew the head, body, arms, and legs together, as outlined in the instructions on page 17. Remember to leave the second leg and the second arm (the pieces with "splits") unstuffed.

Fold the gut pocket in half widthwise, with right sides facing inward, and whipstitch the sides together. Whipstitch the top edges of the pocket just below the outer edges of the gap on the upper body, so that the seams of the pocket are at the top and bottom of the gap and the right side of the knitting is on the inside of the pocket.

Fold the stomach piece in half, with the right side on the outside, to form a semicircle. Whipstitch the curved seam, stuffing the piece lightly as you work. Whipstitch the long seam of the intestine piece and attach it to one corner of the stomach.

Sew the inner leg in the same way as the other leg pieces and stuff lightly. Insert the inner leg into the main unstuffed leg. Secure the split on the outer leg to the inner leg. Work a row of chain stitch on the inner part of the leg in purple. Make a few straight stitches in beige over the edge, as shown in the photograph.

Sew the inner arm piece together in a similar way to the other arm pieces and stuff lightly. Insert the inner arm into the main unstuffed arm. Carefully pull out the yarn threaded through the final row of stitches and whipstitch the edge to the inner arm. Finish the top of the arm as for the first arm. Complete the top of the arm as outlined in the general instructions.

Using cream yarn, embroider the ribs in chain stitch, using the photograph as a guide.

Sew the green bugle beads to the hands and feet to represent the nails.

Using dark gray yarn, embroider a ring of chain stitch for the eye socket. Using the same yarn, embroider the nose in satin stitch, working a straight stitch down the sides to tidy up the edges. Using black yarn, embroider the mouth in satin stitch, using vertical stitches. Work around the mouth in chain stitch. Using a separated strand of bright red yarn, embroider the blood trickling from the mouth in chain stitch. Sew three small white bugle beads onto the mouth to represent the teeth. Using dark red yarn, sew the eye bead to the head, using a single, long straight stitch.

Shade in the eye socket, using the gray crayon.

For the hair, cut 16 lengths, each 8 inches (20 cm) long, of yellow mohair yarn and divide them into two bunches of eight lengths. Sew the center of the bunches to each side of the head.

JACKET
LEFT SIDE
MAKE 1
- Cast on 14 sts in rust 4-ply.
- 1st row: K.
- Next row: K3, P11.
- Rep last 2 rows 10 more times.
- Next row: K2, M1, K to end. (15 sts)
- Next row: K3, P to end.
- Next row: K.
- Next row: K3, P to end.
- Rep last 4 rows 1 more time. (16 sts)
- Next row: K6, P5, K5.
- Next row: K3, P2, K5, P6.
- Next row: K6, P1, K3, P1, K5.
- Next row: K3, P2, K1, P3, K1, P6.
- Rep last 2 rows 1 more time.
- Next row: K.
- Next row: K3, P13.
- Rep last 2 rows 3 more times.
- K 5 rows.
- Bind off.

RIGHT SIDE
MAKE 1
- Cast on 14 sts in rust 4-ply.
- 1st row: K.
- Next row: P11, K3.
- Rep last 2 rows 10 more times.
- Next row: K to last 2 sts, M1, K2. (15 sts)
- Next row: P to last 3 sts, K3.
- Next row: K.
- Next row: P to last 3 sts, K3.

- Rep last 4 rows 1 more time. (16 sts)
- Next row: K5, P5, K6.
- Next row: P6, K5, P2, K3.
- Next row: K5, P1, K3, P1, K6.
- Next row: P6, K1, P3, K1, P2, K3.
- Rep last 2 rows 1 more time.
- Next row: K.
- Next row: P13, K3.
- Rep last 2 rows 3 more times.
- K 5 rows.
- Bind off.

BACK
MAKE 1
- Cast on 22 sts in rust 4-ply yarn.
- Work 22 rows in st st, beg with a K row.
- Next row: K2, M1, K to last 2 sts, M1, K2. (24 sts)
- Work 3 rows in st st, beg with a P row.
- Rep last 4 rows 1 more time. (26 sts)
- Work 14 rows in st st, beg with a K row.
- K 5 rows.
- Bind off.

LEFT SLEEVE
MAKE 1
- Cast on 14 sts in rust 4-ply yarn.
- Work 24 rows in st st, beg with a P row.
- Bind off.

RIGHT SLEEVE
MAKE 1
- Cast on 14 sts in rust 4-ply yarn.
- Work 31 rows in st st, beg with a P row.
- Bind off.

MAKING UP
Sew the long seams of the sleeves, using mattress stitch. With the two side and back pieces right sides outward, whipstitch ⅝ inch (15 mm) along each side of the top edges to form the shoulder seams. Sew the sides using running stitch, leaving the top 1¼ inches (3 cm) open to form the armholes. Insert the sleeves into the armholes of the main piece and whipstitch around the armholes from the inside. For the holes, work a flattened circle of chain stitch in rust 4-ply yarn where you want the holes to be, then cut your knitting on the inside of the shape.

PANTS
MAKE 1
- Cast on 20 sts in variegated gray 4-ply yarn for first leg.
- Work 16 rows in st st, beg with a K row.
- Break yarn and leave sts on needle.

- Cast on 20 sts for second leg.
- Work 16 rows in st st, beg with a K row.
- Next row: K 20 sts from second leg, then 20 sts from first leg. (40 sts)
- Work 17 rows in st st, beg with a P row.
- Next row: [K2, P2] to end.
- Rep last row 3 more times.
- Bind off, keeping to the K2, P2 pattern.

MAKING UP
Using mattress stitch, sew the back seam of the pants so that the lowest part of the seam is level with the crotch. Then sew the two inside leg seams, again using mattress stitch. Using matching yarn, work a border of chain stitch about ⅜ inch (1 cm) up from the lower edge of one leg. Trim off the knitting below this to form a frayed edging. Work the holes in the same way as described for the jacket, left.

Rat

THE DOLL
BODY AND HEAD
FIRST SIDE
MAKE 1

- Cast on 18 sts in dark brown.
- 1st row: K to last 3 sts, ssk, K1. (17 sts)
- Next row: P2tog, P to end. (16 sts)
- Next row: K1, k2tog, K to last 3 sts, ssk, K1. (14 sts)
- Next row: P2tog, P to end. (13 sts)
- Rep last 4 rows 1 more time. (8 sts)
- Bind off.

SECOND SIDE
MAKE 1

- Cast on 18 sts in dark brown.
- 1st row: K1, k2tog, K to end. (17 sts)
- Next row: P to last 2 sts, p2tog. (16 sts)
- Next row: K1, k2tog, K to last 3 sts, ssk, K1. (14 sts)
- Next row: P to last 2 sts, p2tog. (13 sts)
- Rep last 4 rows 1 more time. (8 sts)
- Bind off.

EARS
MAKE 1

- Using the crochet hook, make a 4-chain crochet chain in dark brown.

TAIL
MAKE 1

- Using the crochet hook, make a 2³⁄₄-inch-long (7-cm) crochet chain in dark brown.

MAKING UP
Place the two body and head pieces right sides together and whipstitch the edges, leaving a gap at the lower edge for turning and stuffing. Turn the rat the right way out, stuff, and close the gap.

With black yarn, embroider two French knots for the eyes. Using a separated strand of white yarn, work a ring of chain stitch around each French knot. Using black yarn, work a French knot for the nose. Add the whiskers, using cream thread.

Form the ear chains into small loops and fasten to the head, using the yarn "tails."

Thread one yarn tail up through the tail and use the yarn tails to sew the rat's tail to the end of the body.

Frankenstein's MONSTER

Y ou probably know (as any self-respecting horror fan should) that Frankenstein isn't the name of the monster, but that of his creator. Sewn and patched together, this woolly frightener follows the prescription from the cult 1931 movie: squared-off head, vacant glare, and horrible green pallor. He's finished off with a bolt through his neck—this is a man-made monster, after all. Poignantly, he's smartly dressed—in a classic dark suit, just a little too small. Really, he'd just like to fit in with the crowd.

PEDIGREE

1818 *Frankenstein* the novel is conceived by Mary Shelley as the result of one of those after-dinner games that everyone regrets in the morning.

1910 The first Frankenstein-themed moving picture is made in the Bronx in New York (featuring a somewhat unconvincing monster).

1931 The movie *Frankenstein* (right), James Whales' classic and the model for all its successors, appears in the movie theaters. And the rest is history . . .

UNIVERSAL PRESENTA

FRANKENSTEIN

CON
COLIN CLIVE
MAE CLARKE
JOHN BOLES
BORIS KARLOFF

BASADA EN LA HISTORIA DE MARY WOLLSTONE CROFT SHELLEY

DIRIGIDA POR **JAMES WHALE**

Frankenstein's MONSTER

Huge, ugly, and patched together from odd body parts, Frankenstein's monster has been driven by sorrow and loneliness to commit the most terrible crimes. Although he's not a pretty face, the monster has a kinder side to him; most of all, he wants to meet someone who will accept him for himself. Knit your own version and show him that at least you love him for who he is.

YOU WILL NEED

1 skein green DK yarn; 225 yd (206 m) per 3.5 oz (100 g)

1 skein black DK yarn; 225 yd (206 m) per 3.5 oz (100 g)

Small amounts of white and red DK yarns

1 skein dark brown DK yarn; 225 yd (206 m) per 3.5 oz (100 g)

1 oz/30 g polyester toy filling

Cream sewing thread

A 1½-in (40-mm) nut and bolt

A ½-in (13-mm) dark brown button

A ½-in (13-mm) dark red button

A piece of Velcro tape in beige, measuring 1 x ³⁄₈ in (2.5 x 1 cm)

A piece of Velcro tape in beige, measuring 2 x ¾ in (5 x 2 cm)

Two ½-in (13-mm) snap fasteners

YOU WILL ALSO NEED

A pair of U.S. 2/3 (3 mm) knitting needles

A pair of U.S. 2 (2.75 mm) knitting needles

A yarn needle to sew your items together

An embroidery needle

An ordinary sewing needle

THE DOLL
HEAD
FRONT
MAKE 1
- Using U.S. 2/3 (3 mm) needles, cast on 10 sts in green.
- 1st row: Inc1, K7, inc1, K1. (12 sts)
- Work 3 rows in st st, beg with a P row.
- Next row: K2, M1, K to last 2 sts, M1, K2. (14 sts)
- Next row: P.
- Rep last 2 rows 2 more times. (18 sts)
- * Work 15 rows in st st, beg with a K row.
- Next row: P2tog, P14, p2tog. (16 sts)
- Bind off.

BACK
MAKE 1
- Using U.S. 2/3 (3 mm) needles, cast on 10 sts in green.
- 1st row: Inc1, K7, inc1, K1. (12 sts)
- Work 3 rows in st st, beg with a P row.
- Next row: K2, M1, K1, yo, k2tog, K3, yo, k2tog, M1, K2. (14 sts)
- Next row: P.
- Next row: K2, M1, K to last 2 sts, M1, K2. (16 sts)
- Next row: P.
- Rep last 2 rows 1 more time. (18 sts)
- Cont as for front from * to end.

EARS
MAKE 2
- Using U.S. 2 (2.75 mm) needles, cast on 8 sts in green.
- 1st row: K2tog, K4, ssk. (6 sts)
- Next row: P2tog, P2, p2tog. (4 sts)
- Next row: K2tog, ssk. (2 sts)

- Next row: P2tog.
- Break yarn and pull it through rem st.

UPPER BODY
The upper body is knitted from the top to the bottom.
FRONT
MAKE 1
- Using U.S. 2/3 (3 mm) needles, cast on 20 sts in green.
- Work 6 rows in st st, beg with a K row.
- Next row: Cast on 4 sts, K to end. (24 sts)
- Next row: Cast on 4 sts, P to end. (28 sts)
- Work 6 rows in st st, beg with a K row.
- Next row: K4, k2tog, K to last 6 sts, ssk, K4. (26 sts)
- Work 5 rows in st st, beg with a P row.
- Rep last 6 rows 2 more times. (22 sts)
- Next row: K.
- Next row: P4, K14, P4.
- Next row: Bind off 4 sts, K to last 4 sts, bind off 4 sts. (14 sts)
- Break yarn and rejoin it to WS of work.
- Work 5 rows in st st, beg with a P row.
- Bind off.

BACK
MAKE 1
- Using U.S. 2/3 (3 mm) needles, cast on 20 sts in green.
- Work 6 rows in st st, beg with a K row.
- Next row: K2, k2tog, K to last 4 sts, ssk, K2. (18 sts)
- Work 5 rows in st st, beg with a P row.
- Rep last 6 rows 2 more times. (14 sts)
- Bind off.

LOWER BODY
FRONT
MAKE 1
- Using U.S. 2/3 (3 mm) needles, cast on 14 sts in green.
- Work 6 rows in st st, beg with a K row.
- Next row: Cast on 4 sts, K to end. (18 sts)
- Next row: Cast on 4 sts, P to end. (22 sts)
- Work 7 rows in st st, beg with a K row.
- Next row: P4, K14, P4.
- Next row: Bind off 4 sts, K to last 4 sts, bind off 4 sts. (14 sts)
- Break yarn and rejoin it to WS of work.
- Work 5 rows in st st, beg with a P row.
- Bind off.

BACK
MAKE 1
- Using U.S. 2/3 (3 mm) needles, cast on 14 sts in green.
- Work 8 rows in st st, beg with a K row.
- Bind off.

LEGS
MAKE 2
- Using U.S. 2/3 (3 mm) needles, cast on 30 sts in green.
- Work 6 rows in st st, beg with a K row.
- Next row: K6, bind off 18 sts,
- K to end. (12 sts)
- Work 19 rows in st st, beg with a P row.
- Bind off.

ARMS
MAKE 2
- Using U.S. 2/3 (3 mm) needles, cast on 4 sts in green.
- Work 4 rows in st st, beg with a K row.
- Next row: Cast on 3 sts, K to end. (7 sts)
- Next row: Cast on 3 sts, P to end. (10 sts)
- Work 28 rows in st st, beg with a K row.
- Next row: K2, M1, K3, M1, K3, M1, K2. (13 sts)
- Work 3 rows in st st, beg with a P row.
- Next row: K2, k2tog, K5, ssk, K2. (11 sts)
- Next row: P2tog, P7, p2tog. (9 sts)
- Bind off.

MAKING UP AND DECORATING
Sew the head, body, leg, and arm pieces together, as outlined in the instructions on page 17.

Whipstitch the ears to the sides of the head.

Using black yarn, work two French knots for the eyes. Make a semicircle of chain stitch around the lower half of each French knot, using white yarn. Work a straight stitch for the mouth, using a separated strand of red yarn. Using another separated strand of red yarn, make the scar in chain stitch. Work a series of straight stitches over the scar, using a separated strand of green yarn. Work the brows, nose, and inner cheeks in chain stitch, using green yarn. Work a series of straight stitches for the hair, using black yarn.

Using the gray crayon, add shadows beneath the eyes.

Put the bolt through the back of the head at the side of the "neck" and secure it with the nut at the other side.

JACKET
The two front sides and the back of the jacket are knitted as one piece, from the lower edge to the neck edge.
MAKE 1
- Using U.S. 2/3 (3 mm) needles, cast on 48 sts in black.
- K 2 rows.
- Next row: K2, P to last 2 sts, K2.
- Next row: K.
- Rep last 2 rows 9 more times.
- Next row: K2, P to last 2 sts, K2.
- Next row: K14, then turn and work on only these sts, leaving rem sts on needle.
- Next row: P12, K2.
- Next row: K.
- Rep last 2 rows 2 more times.
- Next row: P12, K2.
- Next row: Bind off 3 sts, K to end. (11 sts)
- Break yarn and leave sts on needle.
- Rejoin yarn to rem 34 sts on needle on RS of work.
- Next row: K20, then turn and work on only these sts, leaving rem sts on needle.
- Work 8 rows in st st, beg with a P row.
- Break yarn and leave sts on needle.
- Rejoin yarn to rem 14 sts on needle on RS of work.
- Next row: K.
- Next row: K2, P12.
- Rep last 2 rows 3 more times.
- Next row: Bind off 3 sts, K to end, then K across the other 31 sts on needle. (42 sts)
- Next row: K11, [k2tog] 4 times, K4, [ssk] 4 times, K11. (34 sts)
- K 3 rows.
- Bind off.

SLEEVES
MAKE 2
- Using U.S. 2/3 (3 mm) needles, cast on 14 sts in black.
- Work 24 rows in st st, beg with a K row.
- Bind off.

MAKING UP
With the right sides of the jacket together, whipstitch the shoulder seams. Sew the sleeve seams, using mattress stitch. Insert each sleeve into an armhole of the main piece and whipstitch them from the inside. Overlap the left border over the right border of the jacket and sew on one of the buttons. Sew the other button above this on the right border.

PANTS
MAKE 1
- Using U.S. 2/3 (3 mm) needles, cast on 20 sts in dark brown for first leg.
- Work 12 rows in st st, beg with a K row.
- Next row: K3, bind off 3 sts, K to end. (17 sts)
- Next row: P14, turn and cast on 3 sts, turn again, and P to end. (20 sts)
- Work 4 rows in st st, beg with a K row.
- Break yarn and leave sts on needle.
- Cast on 20 sts for second leg.
- Work 8 rows in st st, beg with a K row.
- Next row: K12, bind off 3 sts, K to end. (17 sts)
- Next row: P5, turn and cast on 3 sts, turn again, and P to end. (20 sts)
- Work 8 rows in st st, beg with a K row.

- Next row: K 20 sts from second leg, then 20 sts from first leg. (40 sts)
- Work 9 rows in st st, beg with a P row.
- Next row: K29, bind off 3 sts, K to end. (37 sts)
- Next row: P8, turn and cast on 3 sts, turn again, and P to end. (40 sts)
- Work 4 rows in st st, beg with a K row.

- Next row: [K2, P2] to end.
- Rep last row 3 more times.
- Bind off, keeping to the K2, P2 pattern.

MAKING UP
Using mattress stitch, sew the back seam of the pants so that the lowest part of the seam is level with the crotch. Then sew the two inside leg seams, again using mattress stitch.

Zombie COP

This isn't the friendly, doughnut-loving lunk you're familiar with from untold numbers of cop shows—this bloated little monster has a taste for altogether less wholesome fare. Wielding a truncheon fashioned from a thighbone, wearing a rotten old uniform covered in gore, and with fuzzy features in an advanced state of puffy decay, there are plenty of clues to tell you that Zombie Cop's law-enforcement days are long over. It's not just the bad guys who'll be running away as fast as they can.

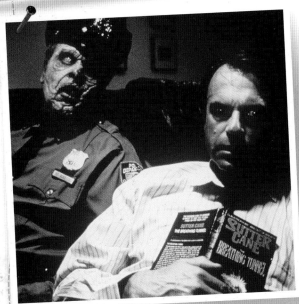

PEDIGREE

1995 *In The Mouth of Madness* (left), directed by John Carpenter, features some seriously scary zombie cop action.

1996 The game "Resident Evil" is released, spawning a franchise covering everything from movies to soft toys. Its lurching zombie policemen are among the most frightening of the genre.

2010 *The Walking Dead* is adapted from black-and-white comic book to a television series. It features undead cops, but its complex police hero, Rick Grimes, hasn't turned zombie . . . yet.

Zombie COP

Spotty, goofy, decomposed . . . you name it. This law enforcer is hardly a looker, even by zombie standards—that bruised, swollen eye is the icing on the cake. There are plenty of reminders of his day job, however, including some effective little handcuffs and a fine, peaked uniform hat.

YOU WILL NEED

1 skein pale brown DK yarn; 225 yd (206 m) per 3.5 oz (100 g)

Very small amounts of red and green DK yarns

Small amounts of black and cream DK yarns

Very small amount of black mohair or mohair/silk yarn

1 skein pale blue DK yarn; 225 yd (206 m) per 3.5 oz (100 g)

1 skein royal blue DK yarn; 225 yds (206 m) per 3.5 oz (100 g)

1 skein mid-blue DK yarn; 225 yd (206 m) per 3.5 oz (100 g)

1 oz/30 g polyester toy filling

Cream sewing thread

Three small white glass bugle beads

Two small dark gray buttons

A small metal star brad

A small metal button

Two ¾-in (17-mm) metal toggle rings joined with a short length of chain for the handcuffs

A 2½-in (6-cm) length of plastic drinking straw

A piece of Velcro tape in beige, measuring 1 x ⅜ in (2.5 x 1 cm)

A piece of Velcro tape in beige, measuring 2 x ¾ in (5 x 2 cm)

Two ½-in (13-mm) snap fasteners

YOU WILL ALSO NEED

A pair of U.S. 2/3 (3 mm) knitting needles

A yarn needle to sew your items together

An embroidery needle

An ordinary sewing needle

A gray crayon

THE DOLL
HEAD
BACK
MAKE 1
- Cast on 18 sts in pale brown.
- 1st row: Inc1, K to last 2 sts, inc1, K1. (20 sts)
- Work 7 rows in st st, beg with a P row. *
- Next row: K2, k2tog, K to last 4 sts, ssk, K2. (18 sts)
- Next row: P.
- Rep last 2 rows 2 more times. (14 sts)
- Work 6 rows in st st, beg with a K row.
- Next row: K2, [k2tog] twice, K2, [ssk] twice, K2. (10 sts)
- Next row: P2tog, P to last 2 sts, p2tog. (8 sts)
- Bind off.

FRONT
MAKE 1
- Work as for back until *.
- Next row: K2, k2tog, K5, [K1, P1, K1] into next 2 sts, turn and P6 sts, turn again and K6 sts, turn again and P6 sts, turn again and k2tog, K2, ssk, K5, ssk, K2. (20 sts)
- Next row: P.
- Next row: K2, k2tog, K4, k2tog, ssk, K4, ssk, K2. (16 sts)
- Next row: P.
- Next row: K2, k2tog, K to last 4 sts, ssk, K2. (14 sts)
- Work 7 rows in st st, beg with a P row.
- Next row: K2, [k2tog] twice, K2, [ssk] twice, K2. (10 sts)
- Next row: P2tog, P to last 2 sts, p2tog. (8 sts)
- Bind off.

EAR
MAKE 1
- Cast on 5 sts in pale brown.
- 1st row: K.
- Next row: P2tog, K1, p2tog. (3 sts)
- Next row: S1, k2tog, psso.
- Break yarn and pull it through rem st.

UPPER BODY
The upper body is knitted from the top to the bottom.

FRONT
MAKE 1
- Cast on 20 sts in pale brown.
- Work 6 rows in st st, beg with a K row.
- Next row: Cast on 4 sts, K to end. (24 sts)
- Next row: Cast on 4 sts, P to end. (28 sts)
- Work 4 rows in st st, beg with a K row.
- Next row: K4, k2tog, K to last 6 sts, ssk, K4. (26 sts)
- Work 5 rows in st st, beg with a P row.
- Rep last 6 rows 2 more times. (22 sts)
- Next row: K.
- Next row: P4, K14, P4.
- Next row: Bind off 4 sts, K to last 4 sts, bind off 4 sts. (14 sts)
- Break yarn and rejoin it to WS of work.
- Work 5 rows in st st, beg with a P row.
- Bind off.

BACK
MAKE 1
- Cast on 20 sts in pale brown.
- Work 4 rows in st st, beg with a K row.
- Next row: K2, k2tog, K to last 4 sts, ssk, K2. (18 sts)
- Work 5 rows in st st, beg with a P row.

- Rep last 6 rows 2 more times. (14 sts)
- Work 2 rows in st st, beg with a K row.
- Bind off.

LOWER BODY
FRONT
MAKE 1
- Cast on 14 sts in pale brown.
- Work 6 rows in st st, beg with a K row.
- Next row: Cast on 4 sts, K to end. (18 sts)
- Next row: Cast on 4 sts, P to end. (22 sts)
- Work 7 rows in st st, beg with a K row.
- Next row: P4, K14, P4.
- Next row: Bind off 4 sts, K to last 4 sts, bind off 4 sts. (14 sts)
- Break yarn and rejoin it to WS of work.
- Work 5 rows in st st, beg with a P row.
- Bind off.

BACK
MAKE 1
- Cast on 14 sts in pale brown.
- Work 8 rows in st st.
- Bind off.

LEGS
MAKE 2
- Cast on 28 sts in pale brown.
- Work 6 rows in st st, beg with a K row.
- Next row: K6, bind off 16 sts, K to end. (12 sts)
- Work 21 rows in st st, beg with a P row.
- Bind off.

ARMS
MAKE 2
- Cast on 4 sts in pale brown.
- Work 4 rows in st st, beg with a K row.
- Next row: Cast on 3 sts, K to end. (7 sts)
- Next row: Cast on 3 sts, P to end. (10 sts)
- Work 24 rows in st st, beg with a K row.
- Next row: K2, M1, K3, M1, K3, M1, K2. (13 sts)
- Work 3 rows in st st, beg with a P row.
- Next row: K2, k2tog, K to last 4 sts, ssk, K2. (11 sts)
- Next row: P2tog, P to last 2 sts, p2tog. (9 sts)
- Bind off.

MAKING UP AND DECORATING
Sew the head, body, arms, and legs together as outlined in the instructions on page 17.

Using red yarn, work a few rows of chain stitch on one arm for the wound. Work a row of chain stitch around the wound, using a separated strand of green yarn.

Sew the ear in place.

Work a French knot for one of the eyes, using black yarn. Using green yarn, work a ring of chain stitch around the French knot. Using pale brown yarn, work two short rows of chain stitch for the bruised eye. Make a straight stitch across the middle of the two rows, using a separated strand of red yarn. Work a group of seven French knots in pale brown yarn on one cheek. On the other cheek, work three straight

stitches, using a separated strand of red yarn. Make a few straight stitches over one of these, using a separated strand of black yarn. Work the outline of the mouth in chain stitch, using black yarn. Work the center of the mouth in satin stitch, keeping your stitches vertical. Work around one side of the mouth in chain stitch, using a separated strand of red yarn. Sew the three white bugle beads in place for the teeth.

Shade in the bruised eye socket, using the gray crayon.

For the hair, cut ten lengths of black mohair yarn, each 2¾ inches (7 cm) long. Divide the yarn into two bunches of five lengths and secure at the centers to each side of the head.

SHIRT
MAKE 1
- Cast on 42 sts in pale blue.
- K 2 rows.
- Next row: K2, P to last 2 sts, K2.
- Next row: K.
- Rep last 2 rows 5 more times.
- Next row: K2, P to last 2 sts, K2.
- Next row: K11, then turn and work on only these 11 sts, leaving rem sts on needle.
- Next row: P to last 2 sts, K2.
- Next row: K.
- Rep last 2 rows 5 more times.
- Break yarn and leave sts on needle.
- Rejoin yarn to rem sts on RS of work.
- Next row: K20, then turn and work on these only 20 sts, leaving 11 rem sts on needle.
- Work 12 rows in st st, beg with a P row.

- Break yarn and leave sts on needle.
- Rejoin yarn to rem sts on RS of work.
- Next row: K.
- Next row: K2, P to end.
- Rep last 2 rows 5 more times.
- Next row: K.
- Now work across all 42 sts.
- Next row: Bind off 3 sts, K to end. (39 sts)
- Rep last row 1 more time. (36 sts)
- K 4 rows.
- Bind off.

FIRST SLEEVE
MAKE 1
- Cast on 18 sts in pale blue.
- 1st row: K.
- Work 12 rows in st st, beg with a K row.
- Bind off.

SECOND SLEEVE
MAKE 1
- Cast on 18 sts in pale blue.
- Work 10 rows in st st, beg with a K row.
- Bind off.

MAKING UP
On the second sleeve, work a row of chain stitch across the sleeve a few rows up from the bound-off edge. Trim your knitting beneath this stitching and unravel the yarn a little so that it looks loopy. With the right sides of the shirt facing outward, whipstitch the front to the back at the shoulders. Sew the sleeve seams, using mattress stitch. Insert the sleeves into the armholes of the main piece and whipstitch them from the inside. Overlap the left border over the right border of the shirt and sew on one of the small buttons. Sew the other button below this on the right border. Fasten the metal brad in place on the chest of the shirt. Using red yarn, work a combination of French knots, some with straight stitches coming out in a star pattern, to represent splattered blood.

PANTS
MAKE 1
- Cast on 20 sts in royal blue for first leg.
- 1st row: K.

- Work 20 rows in st st, beg with a K row.
- Break yarn and leave sts on needle.
- Cast on 20 sts for second leg.
- 1st row: K.
- Work 16 rows in st st, beg with a K row.
- Next row: K 20 sts from second leg, then 20 sts from first leg. (40 sts)
- Work 15 rows in st st, beg with a P row.
- Next row: K2, P2 to end.
- Rep last row 2 more times.
- Bind off, keeping to the K2, P2 pattern.

MAKING UP
Using mattress stitch, sew the back seam of the pants so that the lowest part of the seam is level with the crotch. Then sew the two inside leg seams, again, using mattress stitch.

HAT
The hat is knitted in two main parts—the side band and the tip. The peak is knitted onto the side band once the two main parts have been sewn together.

SIDE BAND
MAKE 1
- Cast on 26 sts in black.
- K 2 rows.
- Break yarn and join mid-blue yarn.
- Next row: P.
- Next row: K1, [inc1] to last st, K1. (50 sts)
- Work 3 rows in st st, beg with a P row.
- Bind off pwise.

TIP
MAKE 1
- Cast on 10 sts in mid-blue.
- 1st row: K1, inc1, K to last 2 sts, inc1, K1. (12 sts)
- Next row: P.
- Next row: K1, M1, K to last st, M1, K1. (14 sts)
- Next row: P.
- Rep last 2 rows 3 more times. (20 sts)
- Work 4 rows in st st, beg with a K row.
- Next row: K1, k2tog, K to last 3 sts, ssk, K1. (18 sts)
- Next row: P.
- Rep last 2 rows 3 more times. (12 sts)
- Next row: K1, k2tog, K to last 3 sts, ssk, K1. (10 sts)
- Bind off kwise.

Sew the short sides of the side band to form a circle; whipstitch the tip in place from the inside, so that the rows of knitting lie across the width of the hat.

PEAK
MAKE 1
- With the RS of the hat facing, using black yarn, pick up and knit 12 sts across the lower edge of the front of the side band, one side to the other.

- Next row: P.
- Next row: K1, k2tog, K to last 3 sts, ssk, K1. (10 sts)
- Next row: P.
- Rep last 2 rows 1 more time. (8 sts)
- Next row: K1, M1, K6, M1, K1. (10 sts)
- Next row: P.
- Next row: K1, M1, K8, M1, K1. (12 sts)
- Bind off kwise.

MAKING UP
Fold the bound-off edge of the peak under. Whipstitch the sides of the peak together and the bound-off edge of the peak to the inside of the hat. Sew the metal button in place.

BOOT
MAKE 1
- Cast on 30 sts in black.
- K 2 rows.
- Work 4 rows in st st, beg with a K row.
- Next row: K8, bind off 14 sts, K to end. (16 sts)
- Work 7 rows in st st, beg with a P row.
- Next row: P.
- Bind off pwise.

MAKING UP
Fold the piece widthwise with the right sides together. Whipstitch the back, lower, and upper seams, then turn the boot right side out.

BONE TRUNCHEON
MAKE 1
- Cast on 10 sts in cream.
- Work 2 rows in st st, beg with a K row.
- Next row: K1, k2tog, K4, ssk, K1. (8 sts)
- Work 15 rows in st st, beg with a P row.
- Next row: K1, M1, K6, M1, K1. (10 sts)
- Next row: P.
- Bind off.

MAKING UP
Fold the piece in half lengthwise, with the right sides on the inside, and whipstitch both ends. Turn the bone right side out, insert the plastic drinking straw, and sew the seam, using mattress stitch. Make a couple of straight stitches at each short edge to create the bone ends.

Village IdIOT

Zombie Rock Star
head and brain

+

Zombie Grave Digger
head

+

Frankenstein's
Monster
upper body

+

Frankenstein's
Monster
arms

Frankenstein's
Monster jacket

+

Classic Zombie
legs

=

Classic Zombie
pants

He may be a couple of cards short of a full deck, but this particular idiot is smart enough to know that two heads are better than one. So he's brought one along with him, clasped securely under his rotten arm. And with his brain (decoratively adorned with chain stitch) sitting loosely in his cranium, he may well need a spare. Every zombie needs one brain to think with and another to eat.

zombie FATaLE

She's pretty well-groomed—for a zombie, that is. Her beehive hairdo is neatly furled and finished with a shiny flower, her crochet dress is set off with a cute pink trim, and even if her face is a little bit of a battleground, she's still boasting a cheerful slash of bright fuchsia lipstick. Under her frock, however, her heart's hanging loose in her chest; the shiny red nails on that single unbandaged hand look a little like claws—and is that a spider on her ladylike fascinator? Ugh, better not offer to buy this gal a drink.

PEDiGrEE

1897 Bram Stoker's *Dracula* features Lucy Westenra, lovely, intelligent, and one of the first female undead, who, after her death, comes back to prey on children. She might have turned evil, but she was never ugly!

1932 The first zombie-themed movie, *White Zombie* (right), is released in the United States. It stars Bela Lugosi, and features an alluring femme fatale-style zombie.

2004 *Shaun of the Dead*, an award-winning zombie comedy, offers its audiences an unusually everyday girl zombie in the girl-in-the-yard scene.

SHE WAS NOT ALIVE... NOR DEAD... *Just a*

WHITE ZOMBIE

Performing his every desire

A VICTOR & EDWARD HALPERIN Production

with BELA *Dracula* LUGOSI

Released by UNITED ARTISTS

Zombie FaTALE

Although she died a while back, that doesn't mean that she's let herself go. Take a look at her charm-hung belt and you'll get the idea. And with all those boys out in Zombie Land, she could easily lose her heart. No worries: You can slip it right back into her chest.

YOU WILL NEED

1 skein pale gray DK yarn; 225 yd (206 m) per 3.5 oz (100 g)

Small amounts of red, pastel pink, white, and sparkly black DK yarns

Very small amounts of black, green, cream, dark gray, and bright pink DK yarns

Small amounts of yellow and black mohair or mohair/silk yarns

1 skein mid-pink DK yarn; 225 yd (206 m) per 3.5 oz (100 g)

1 skein mauve DK yarn; 225 yd (206 m) per 3.5 oz (100 g)

1 oz/30 g polyester toy filling

Cream sewing thread

Six red bugle beads

A red flower button

A small bronze metal skull charm with jump ring

A small white feather charm with jump ring

A small pale yellow bow

Three 5/8-in (15-mm) brass rings

A piece of black netting measuring 1 3/4 x 6 1/4 in (4.5 x 16 cm)

Two 1/4-in (5-mm) black beads

A piece of Velcro tape in white, measuring 1 x 3/8 in (2.5 x 1 cm)

A piece of Velcro tape in white, measuring 2 x 3/4 in (5 x 2 cm)

Two 1/2-in (13-mm) snap fasteners

YOU WILL ALSO NEED

A pair of U.S. 2/3 (3 mm) knitting needles

A size U.S. D-3 (3.25 mm) or similar size crochet hook

A yarn needle to sew your items together

An embroidery needle

An ordinary sewing needle

A green crayon

THE DOLL
HEAD
MAKE 2 PIECES
- Cast on 6 sts in pale gray.
- 1st row: Inc1, K to last 2 sts, inc1, K1. (8 sts)
- Next row: P.
- Rep last 2 rows 1 more time. (10 sts)
- Next row: K2, M1, K to last 2 sts, M1, K2. (12 sts)
- Next row: P.
- Rep last 2 rows 2 more times. (16 sts)
- Work 10 rows in st st, beg with a K row.
- Next row: K2, k2tog, K8, ssk, K2. (14 sts)
- Next row: P2tog, P10, p2tog. (12 sts)
- Bind off.

UPPER BODY
The upper body is knitted from the top to the bottom.

FRONT
MAKE 1
- Cast on 14 sts in pale gray.
- Work 6 rows in st st, beg with a K row.
- Next row: Cast on 4 sts, K to end. (18 sts)
- Next row: Cast on 4 sts, P to end. (22 sts)
- Work 2 rows in st st, beg with a K row.
- Next row: K11, then turn and work on only these 11 sts, leaving rem 11 sts on needle.
- Next row: K1, P10.
- Next row: K.
- Next row: K1, P10.
- Rep last 2 rows 1 more time.
- Next row: K4, k2tog, K5. (10 sts)
- Break yarn and rejoin it to rem 11 sts on RS of work.
- Next row: K.
- Next row: P10, K1.

- Rep last 2 rows 2 more times.
- Next row: K5, ssk, K4. (10 sts)
- Now work across all 20 sts.
- Next row: P2tog, P16, p2tog. (18 sts)
- Work 4 rows in st st, beg with a K row.
- Next row: K4, M1, K to last 4 sts, M1, K2. (20 sts)
- Next row: P.
- Rep last 2 rows 1 more time. (22 sts)
- Work 3 rows in st st, beg with a K row.
- Next row: P4, K14, P4.
- Next row: Bind off 4 sts, K to last 4 sts, bind off 4 sts. (14 sts)
- Break yarn and rejoin it to WS of work.
- Work 5 rows in st st, beg with a P row.
- Bind off.

BACK
MAKE 1
- Cast on 14 sts in pale gray.
- Work 8 rows in st st, beg with a K row.
- Next row: K2, k2tog, K6, ssk, K2. (12 sts)
- Next row: P2tog, P8, p2tog. (10 sts)
- Work 4 rows in st st, beg with a K row.
- Next row: K2, M1, K to last 2 sts, M1, K2. (12 sts)
- Next row: P.
- Rep last 2 rows 1 more time. (14 sts)
- Work 4 rows in st st, beg with a K row.
- Bind off.

LOWER BODY
FRONT
MAKE 1
- Cast on 14 sts in pale gray.

- Work 6 rows in st st, beg with a K row.
- Next row: Cast on 4 sts, K to end. (18 sts)
- Next row: Cast on 4 sts, P to end. (22 sts)
- Work 7 rows in st st, beg with a K row.
- Next row: P4, K14, P4.
- Next row: Bind off 4 sts, K to last 4 sts, bind off 4 sts. (14 sts)
- Break yarn and rejoin it to WS of work.
- Work 5 rows in st st, beg with a P row.
- Bind off.

BACK
MAKE 1
- Cast on 14 sts in pale gray.
- Work 8 rows in st st, beg with a K row.
- Bind off.

CHEST POCKET FOR HEART
MAKE 1
- Cast on 6 sts in pale gray.
- Work 4 rows in st st, beg with a K row.
- Next row: K1, M1, K to last st, M1, K1. (8 sts)
- Work 7 rows in st st, beg with a P row.

• Next row: K1, k2tog, K to last
  3 sts, ssk, K1. (6 sts)
• Work 3 rows in st st, beg with
  a P row.
• Bind off.

HEART
MAKE 1
• Cast on 8 sts in red.
• 1st row: Inc1, K to last 2 sts,
  inc1, K1. (10 sts)
• Next row: P.
• Rep last 2 rows 1 more time.
  (12 sts)
• Work 2 rows in st st, beg with
  a K row.
• Next row: K1, k2tog, K2, k2tog,
  K2, ssk, K1. (9 sts)
• Next row: P2tog, P5, p2tog.
  (7 sts)
• Next row: K1, k2tog, K1, ssk,
  K1. (5 sts)
• Next row: P2tog, P1, p2tog.
  (3 sts)
• Break yarn and thread it
  through rem sts.

BLOOD VESSELS
MAKE 2
• Using the crochet hook, work
  a 1-inch-long (2.5-cm) chain in
  red for each blood vessel.

LEGS
MAKE 2
• Cast on 26 sts in pale gray.
• Work 5 rows in st st, beg with
  a K row.
• Next row: P5, bind off 16 sts,
  P to end. (10 sts)
• Work 20 rows in st st, beg with
  a K row.
• Bind off.

ARMS
MAKE 2
• Cast on 4 sts in pale gray.
• Work 4 rows in st st, beg with
  a K row.
• Next row: Cast on 3 sts, K to
  end. (7 sts)
• Next row: Cast on 3 sts, P to
  end. (10 sts)

• Work 26 rows in st st, beg with
  a K row.
• Next row: K1, k2tog, K4, ssk,
  K1. (8 sts)
• Next row: P2tog, P4, p2tog.
  (6 sts)
• Break yarn, thread it through
  rem sts, and secure.

MAKING UP
AND DECORATING
Sew the head, body, arms, and
legs together, as outlined in the
instructions on page 17.

Fold the chest pocket in half
widthwise, with right sides
facing inward, and whipstitch
the sides together. Whipstitch
the top edges of the pocket
to the outer sides of the gap
on the upper body, so that the
seams of the pocket are at
the top and bottom of the gap
and the right side of the knitting
is on the inside of the pocket.

Fold the heart lengthwise so that the right side is facing outward. Pull the yarn tail from the last row somewhat tightly and whipstitch the side and top seams, stuffing the heart lightly as you work. Thread the tail at one end of the two blood vessels up the chain and pull slightly so that the chain curves. Use the tail ends to sew the blood vessels to the top of the heart.

Using a separated strand of black yarn, work a length of chain stitch for the scar on the leg and work a few straight stitches over the scar. Using a separated strand of bright red yarn, work a length of chain stitch for the scar on the arm and work a few straight stitches over the scar, using a separated strand of black yarn.

Sew three red bugle beads to one arm and one foot to represent nails.

Using black yarn, embroider two French knots for the eyes. Using green yarn, work an oval around one eye and, using cream yarn, work an oval around the other eye. Using pale gray yarn, embroider the nose in chain stitch. Using a separated strand of black yarn, make the eyebrows in chain stitch. Using a separated strand of dark gray yarn, work the eyeliner in chain stitch. Using a separated strand of bright pink yarn, make two V-shape stitches, one over the top of the other, for the mouth. Using a separated strand of red yarn, make the blood trickling from the eye and the scar coming up from the mouth in

chain stitch. Make a few straight stitches over the scar, using a separated strand of black yarn. Shade in under one eye and on one foot end, using the green crayon.

Cut the yellow mohair yarn for the hair into twenty 28-inch (70-cm) lengths and gather together in a bunch. Secure the center of the lengths to the top of the head and at each side of the face. Take the yarn bunches at the sides back to the top of the head and secure again. Take the hair down the back of the head, spread slightly, and backstitch across the head from one side to the other, in line with the stitches that have secured the hair to the sides. Bring the hair back up to the top of the head. Wind into an untidy bun and secure. Sew the red flower button in place. Put the brass ring "bracelets" on the arms.

DRESS
BACK
MAKE 1
• Cast on 24 sts in pastel pink.
• Break yarn and join mid-pink yarn.
• Next row: P.

• Next row: K2, [yo, k2tog] to last 2 sts, K2.
• Next row: P.
• Next row: K3, [yo, k2tog] to last st, K1.
• Rep last 4 rows 3 more times.
• Next row: P.
• Next row: K2, [yo, k2tog] to last 2 sts, K2.
• Next row: P2tog, P to last 2 sts, p2tog. (22 sts)

- Rep last 2 rows 3 more times. (16 sts)
- The lower part of the dress will probably look a little uneven at this stage because of the nature of the stitch pattern. But don't worry—this will be sorted once the dress has been sewn together, soaked, and dried (see page 16).
- Next row: K2, [yo, k2tog] to last 2 sts, K2.
- Next row: P.
- Next row: K3, [yo, k2tog] to last st, K1.
- Next row: P. *
- Rep last 4 rows 3 more times.
- K 2 rows.
- Bind off.

FRONT
MAKE 1
- Work as for back until *.
- Rep last 4 rows 1 more time.
- Next row: K2, [yo, k2tog] twice, K2, then turn and work on only these 8 sts just worked, leaving rem 8 sts on needle.

- Next row: K2, P6.
- Next row: K3, [yo, k2tog twice, K1.
- Next row: K2, P6.
- Rep last 4 rows 1 more time.
- Next row: K6, ssk. (7 sts)
- Next row: K2tog, K5. (6 sts)
- Bind off.
- Rejoin yarn to rem sts on RS of work.
- Next row: K2, [yo, k2tog] twice, K2. (8 sts)
- Next row: P6, K2.
- Next row: K3, [yo, k2tog] twice, K1.
- Next row: P6, K2.
- Rep last 4 rows 1 more time.
- Next row: K2tog, K6. (7 sts)
- Next row: K5, ssk. (6 sts)
- Bind off.

BELT
MAKE 1
- Using the crochet hook, work a 16-inch (40-cm) crochet chain in sparkly black.

MAKING UP
With the right sides of your pieces facing outward, sew the front to the back of the dress at the shoulders. Sew the side seams, using mattress stitch, leaving a gap of ¾ inch (2 cm)

at the top of each seam to form the armholes. When the dress has been soaked, reshaped, and dried (see page 16), put it on the doll. Thread the skull and feather charms onto the belt, wind the belt twice around the doll's waist, and secure in a knot.

BANDAGE
MAKE 1
- Cast on 11 sts in white.
- Work 14 rows in st st, beg with a K row.
- Next row: K1, k2tog, K5, ssk, K1. (9 sts)
- Next row: P2tog, P5, p2tog. (7 sts)
- Break yarn and thread it through rem sts.

MAKING UP
Pull thread tightly and, with the right sides facing outward, sew the side seam, using mattress stitch. Using white yarn, embroider the bandage markings in chain stitch.

SHOE
MAKE 1
- Cast on 10 sts in sparkly black.
- 1st row: Inc1, K to last 2 sts, inc1, K1. (12 sts)
- Next row: P.
- Rep last 2 rows 2 more times. (16 sts)
- Next row: Inc1, K to last 2 sts, inc1, K1. (18 sts)
- Next row: P7, bind off 4 sts pwise, P to end.
- Work on only 7 sts just knitted, leaving rem sts on needle.
- Work 8 rows in st st, beg with a K row.
- Bind off.

- Break yarn and rejoin it to rem sts on RS of work.
- Work 8 rows in st st, beg with a K row.
- Bind off.

MAKING UP

Fold the shoe piece in half lengthwise, with the right sides together, and whipstitch the back and lower seams. Turn the shoe right side out and then sew on the bow.

HAT

MAKE 1

- Cast on 24 sts in mauve.
- Work 6 rows in st st, beg with a K row.
- Next row: Bind off 10 sts, K4, bind off 10 sts. (4 sts)
- Break yarn and rejoin it to rem sts on WS of work.
- Next row: Inc1 pwise, P1, inc1 pwise, K1. (6 sts)
- Next row: Inc1, K3, inc1, K1. (8 sts)
- Work 3 rows in st st, beg with a P row.
- Next row: K1, k2tog, K2, ssk, K1. (6 sts)
- Next row: P2tog, K2, p2tog. (4 sts)
- Next row: K2tog, ssk. (2 sts)
- Next row: P2tog. (1 st)
- Break yarn and pull it through rem st.
- With RS facing, pick up and K 24 sts along cast-on edge.
- Next row: P.
- Next row: [Inc1] 23 times, K1. (47 sts)
- Work 4 rows in st st, beg with a P row.
- Bind off kwise.

MAKING UP

Sew the back seam of the hat, using mattress stitch. Whipstitch the top part of the hat to the sides from the inside. Using a separated strand of mauve yarn, work a row of running stitch along one long edge of the black netting. Gather it and sew the veil in place just under the brim of the hat, using the same piece of yarn. Round the lower corners of the veil with scissors.

For each of the two spiders, cut four 1½-inch (4-cm) lengths of black mohair yarn. Tie the pieces together at the center with a longer piece of yarn and thread both ends of the longer yarn through the bead. Secure one spider to the brim of the hat so that it hangs down. For the second spider, knot the yarn at the top and take the yarn down through the bead again and use these to secure the spider to the hat. Trim the spiders' legs.

Dracula

Is he a zombie? Hmm. He's undead, that's for sure. But his sleek appearance makes a pleasant change in the motley zombie lineup. Smooth hair slicked back with pomade, a flowing cape with deep yellow accents, and a well-cut vest and pants all make him stand out in this crowd. Don't be deceived: A great line in sophisticated banter and exceptionally white teeth don't mean that this is company that you should be keeping.

PEDIGREE

1845–47 *Varney the Vampire; or, the Feast of Blood* (right) appears as one of the "penny dreadful" serials so popular in the nineteenth century.

1897 Bram Stoker's classic *Dracula* is published, introducing the languid sophisticate so familiar to today's vampire enthusiasts.

1931 Bela Lugosi immortalizes Stoker's antihero on celluloid, setting the standard for vampires ever since.

Dracula

With his pointed ears and a cool pet bat, this visitor to Zombie Land survives on the blood of others—and you can see it trickling out of his mouth. Smartly dressed and sporting an elegant skull-topped cane, he may be a cut above your average zombie—although those pants are looking a little tattered. In short, he is a great addition to the zombie horde.

YOU WILL NEED

1 skein pale green DK yarn; 225 yd (206 m) per 3.5 oz (100 g)

1 skein black DK yarn; 225 yd (206 m) per 3.5 oz (100 g)

Very small amounts of white, red, and purple DK yarns

1 skein teal DK yarn; 225 yd (206 m) per 3.5 oz (100 g)

1 skein pale gray DK yarn; 225 yd (206 m) per 3.5 oz (100 g)

Small amounts of deep yellow and pale brown DK yarns

Cream sewing thread

1 oz/30 g polyester toy filling

Two small cylindrical white glass beads

Three small gray buttons

A 5¼-in (13.5-cm) length of plastic drinking straw

A skull-shaped plastic button

A piece of Velcro tape in beige, measuring 1 x ⅜ in (2.5 x 1 cm)

A piece of Velcro tape in beige, measuring 2 x ¾ in (5 x 2 cm)

Two ½-in (13-mm) snap fasteners

YOU WILL ALSO NEED

A pair of U.S. 2/3 (3 mm) knitting needles

A size U.S. D-3 (3.25 mm) or similar size crochet hook

A yarn needle to sew your items together

An embroidery needle

An ordinary sewing needle

A gray crayon

THE DOLL
HEAD
FRONT
MAKE 1
- Cast on 4 sts in pale green.
- 1st row: Inc1, K1, inc1, K1. (6 sts)
- Next row: P.
- Next row: K2, M1, K to last 2 sts, M1, K2. (8 sts)
- Next row: P.
- Rep last 2 rows 4 more times. (16 sts) *
- Work 12 rows in st st, beg with a K row.
- Next row: K2, k2tog, K8, ssk, K2. (14 sts)
- Next row: P2tog, P10, p2tog. (12 sts)
- Bind off.

BACK
MAKE 1
- Work as for front until *.
- Work 4 rows in st st, beg with a K row.
- Break yarn and join black yarn.
- Work 8 rows in st st, beg with a K row.
- Next row: K2, k2tog, K8, ssk, K2. (14 sts)
- Next row: P2tog, P10, p2tog. (12 sts)
- Bind off.

FIRST EAR
MAKE 1
- Cast on 4 sts in pale green.
- 1st row: Inc1, K3. (5 sts)
- Next row: P.
- Bind off.

SECOND EAR
MAKE 1
- Cast on 4 sts in pale green.
- 1st row: K3, inc1. (5 sts)
- Next row: P.
- Bind off.

UPPER BODY
The upper body is knitted from the top to the bottom.
FRONT
MAKE 1
- Cast on 14 sts in pale green.
- Work 6 rows in st st, beg with a K row.
- Next row: Cast on 4 sts, K to end. (18 sts)
- Next row: Cast on 4 sts, P to end. (22 sts)
- Work 23 rows in st st, beg with a K row.
- Next row: P4, K14, P4.
- Next row: Bind off 4 sts, K to last 4 sts, bind off 4 sts. (14 sts)
- Break yarn and rejoin it to WS of work.
- Work 5 rows in st st, beg with a P row.
- Bind off.

BACK
MAKE 1
- Cast on 14 sts in pale green.
- Work 24 rows in st st, beg with a K row.
- Bind off.

LOWER BODY
FRONT
MAKE 1
- Cast on 14 sts in pale green.
- Work 6 rows in st st, beg with a K row.
- Next row: Cast on 4 sts, K to end. (18 sts)
- Next row: Cast on 4 sts, P to end. (22 sts)
- Work 7 rows in st st, beg with a K row.
- Next row: P4, K14, P4.
- Next row: Bind off 4 sts, K to last 4 sts, bind off 4 sts. (14 sts)
- Break yarn and rejoin it to RS of work.

- Work 5 rows in st st, beg with a P row.
- Bind off.

BACK
MAKE 1
- Cast on 14 sts in pale green.
- Work 8 rows in st st, beg with a K row.
- Bind off.

LEGS
MAKE 2
- Cast on 28 sts in pale green.
- Work 6 rows in st st, beg with a K row.
- Next row: K6, bind off 16 sts, K to end. (12 sts)
- Work 23 rows in st st, beg with a P row.
- Bind off.

ARMS
MAKE 2
- Cast on 4 sts in pale green.
- Work 4 rows in st st, beg with a K row.
- Next row: Cast on 3 sts, K to end. (7 sts)
- Next row: Cast on 3 sts, P to end. (10 sts)
- Work 28 rows in st st, beg with a K row.
- Next row: K1, k2tog, K4, ssk, K1. (8 sts)
- Next row: P2tog, P4, p2tog. (6 sts)
- Break yarn, thread it through rem sts, and secure.

MAKING UP AND DECORATING

Sew the head, body, arms, and legs together as outlined in the instructions on page 17.

Whipstitch the ears in place at the sides of the head. Embroider two French knots for the eyes, using black yarn. Using white yarn, work a ring of chain stitch around each French knot. Using a single separated strand of red yarn, work three straight stitches from the center to the outside of one eye. Using a separated strand of black yarn, make the eyebrows in chain stitch. Embroider the nose in chain stitch, using pale green yarn. Embroider the mouth in chain stitch, using a separated strand of purple yarn. Use a separated strand of red yarn to work the trickles of blood in chain stitch. Sew on the two white glass beads for the teeth.

Shade in one of the eye sockets, using the gray crayon.

Using black yarn, work a few rows in chain stitch to form the front part of the hair and sideboards, using the photograph as a guide.

PANTS
MAKE 1
- Cast on 19 sts in teal for the first leg.
- 1st row: K2, [yo, s1, k2tog, psso, yo, K1] 4 times, K1.
- Next row: P.
- Next row: K1, k2tog, yo, K1, [yo, s1, k2tog, psso, yo, K1] 3 times, yo, s1, K1, psso, K1.
- Next row: P.
- Rep last 4 rows 1 more time.
- Work 4 rows in st st, beg with a K row.
- Break yarn and leave sts on needle.
- Cast on 19 sts for second leg.
- Work 18 rows in st st, beg with a K row.
- Next row: K 19 sts from second leg, then 19 sts from first leg. (38 sts)
- Work 15 rows in st st, beg with a P row.
- Next row: [K2, P2] 9 times.
- Next row: [P2, K2] 9 times.
- Next row: [K2, P2] 9 times.
- Bind off, keeping to the K2, P2 pattern.

MAKING UP
Using mattress stitch, sew the back seam of the pants so that the lowest part of the seam is level with the crotch. Then sew the two inside leg seams, again using mattress stitch.

VEST
MAKE 1
- Cast on 42 sts in pale gray.
- 1st row: K2, P to last 2 sts, K2.
- Next row: K.
- Rep last 2 rows 5 more times.
- Next row: K2, P to last 2 sts, K2.
- Next row: K11, then turn and work on only these 11 sts, leaving rem 31 sts on needle.
- Next row: K2, P7, K2. (11 sts)
- Next row: K2, k2tog, K to end. (10 sts)
- Next row: K2, P to last 2 sts, K2.
- Rep last 2 rows 4 more times. (6 sts)
- Next row: K.
- Next row: K2, P2, K2.
- Bind off and break yarn.
- Rejoin yarn to sts rem on needle on RS of work.
- Next row: K20, then turn and work on only these 20 sts, leaving rem 11 sts on needle.
- Next row: K2, P16, K2.
- Next row: K.
- Rep last 2 rows 5 more times.
- Next row: K.
- Bind off and break yarn.
- Rejoin yarn to 11 sts rem on needle on RS of work.
- Next row: K. (11 sts)
- Next row: K2, P7, K2.
- Next row: K to last 4 sts, ssk, K2. (10 sts)
- Next row: K2, P to last 2 sts, K2.
- Rep last 2 rows 4 more times. (6 sts)
- Next row: K.
- Next row: K2, P2, K2.
- Bind off.

MAKING UP
With the right sides of the vest together, whipstitch the shoulder seams. Overlap the left border over the right border of the vest and sew on the small gray buttons.

CAPE
MAKE 1
- Cast on 28 sts in black.
- K 2 rows.
- Next row: K6, M1, K2, M1, K12, M1, K2, M1, K6. (32 sts)
- Next and every WS row unless stated: P.
- Next RS row: K7, M1, K2, M1, K14, M1, K2, M1, K7. (36 sts)
- Next RS row: K8, M1, K2, M1, K16, M1, K2, M1, K8. (40 sts)
- Next RS row: K9, M1, K2, M1, K18, M1, K2, M1, K9. (44 sts)
- Next RS row: K10, M1, K2, M1, K20, M1, K2, M1, K10. (48 sts)

- Next RS row: K11, M1, K2, M1, K22, M1, K2, M1, K11. (52 sts)
- Next row: P.
- Work 30 rows in st st, beg with a K row.
- K 2 rows.
- Bind off pwise.

- With RS facing, pick up and K 28 sts across top (neck) edge.
- K 14 rows.
- Bind off.

TIES
MAKE 2
- Using the crochet hook, make a 6½-inch (16-cm) chain in deep yellow for each cape tie.

MAKING UP
Weave the yarn tail at one end of each of the ties back into the chain and trim. Use the other yarn tail to secure the tie to the neck edges of the cape.

CANE
MAKE 1
- Cast on 38 sts in pale brown.
- Work 3 rows in st st, beg with a K row.
- Bind off pwise.

MAKING UP
Roll the piece around your length of drinking straw so that the reverse of the stockinette stitch is on the outside. Whipstitch down the long seam and the two ends. Sew the skull button in place.

Bat

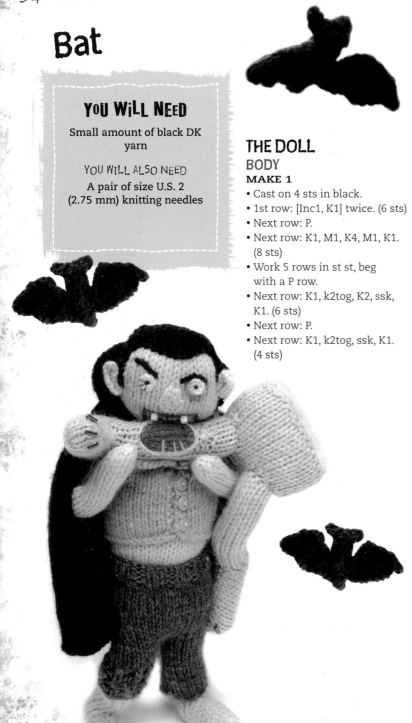

THE DOLL
BODY
MAKE 1
- Cast on 4 sts in black.
- 1st row: [Inc1, K1] twice. (6 sts)
- Next row: P.
- Next row: K1, M1, K4, M1, K1. (8 sts)
- Work 5 rows in st st, beg with a P row.
- Next row: K1, k2tog, K2, ssk, K1. (6 sts)
- Next row: P.
- Next row: K1, k2tog, ssk, K1. (4 sts)
- Next row: [P2tog] twice. (2 sts)
- Next row: K2tog.
- Break yarn and pull it through rem st.

WINGS
The wings are knitted from the lower edge to the top edge.
MAKE 2
- Cast on 20 sts in black.
- 1st row: P2tog, P16, p2tog. (18 sts)
- Next row: K4, p2tog, K6, p2tog, K4. (16 sts)
- Next row: P4, k2tog, P4, k2tog, P4. (14 sts)
- Next row: K2tog, K2, p2tog, K2, p2tog, K2, k2tog. (10 sts)
- Next row: P2tog, k2tog, P2, k2tog, p2tog. (6 sts)
- Next row: K2tog, K2, k2tog. (4 sts)
- Next row: [P2tog] twice. (2 sts)
- Next row: S1, K1, psso. (1 st)
- Break yarn and pull it through rem st.

EARS
MAKE 2
- Cast on 3 sts in black.
- Work 2 rows in st st, beg with a K row.
- Next row: S1, k2tog, psso. (1 st)
- Break yarn and pull it through rem st.

MAKING UP
Fold the body piece in half lengthwise, with right side facing outward, and sew the body seam, stuffing the body slightly as you work. Sew the ears in place. Sew the lower side parts of the wings to the body, using the photograph as a guide.

Mother of the BRiDE

Classic Zombie
head

+

Zombie Fatale legs

+

Zombie Fatale
arms

+

Zombie Fatale
body

Zombie Grave Digger
hat

+

Classic Zombie
jacket

=

Zombie Fatale
dress

Zombie Fatale
heart

Who says the undead can't make an effort for a special day? The Mother of the Bride ran out of time to get her hair done, but she's added an attractive hat to her lively pink 'n' orange ensemble. As it's a cute shade of lilac, everything's blending together wonderfully. Her feet are causing trouble again (no chance of a pedicure when your toes are gangrenous), but her one shoe is set off with a neat bow. The photographs should be very special. Say "cheese."

zombie CHeF

His razor-sharp batterie de cuisine marks this guy out as a professional, whatever his undead status. And he's got the gear to match—jaunty mustache, checkered pants, and a full set of "whites." You have to wonder what it is he's been cooking, however, for them to get in such a state. What a lot of stains—even boiling will never get them out. He's turning people into zombies like it's the house special!

PeDiGRee

1934 The Zombie first enters the dining sphere—with a cocktail. Invented by Donn Beach, an early celebrity restaurateur, the brandy and rum-based drink (left) doesn't turn drinkers into zombies—they just feel that way.

1986 The clunkingly named *Gore-met* is, perhaps surprisingly, the first movie that starred an out-and-out cannibal zombie chef.

1997 The infamous cafeteria zombie scene is aired during the first season of the satirical cartoon, *South Park*—school lunches will never seem the same again.

Zombie CHeF

If you were in any doubt at all that you wouldn't much like this chef preparing your dinner, take a look at those horrible black fingernails. Splashed in blood and goodness knows what else, he's always at the ready with his knife and cleaver to do a little emergency surgery if you are unwise enough to get up close and personal.

YOU WiLL NEED

1 skein light gray DK yarn; 225 yd (206 m) per 3.5 oz (100 g)

Small amounts of red and dark brown DK yarns

1 skein white DK yarn; 225 yd (206 m) per 3.5 oz (100 g)

Very small amounts of black, bright pink, pale green, and dark gray DK yarns

Very small amount of black mohair or mohair/silk yarn

1 skein navy 4-ply yarn; 494 yd (452 m) per 3.5 oz (100 g)

1 skein cream 4-ply yarn; 494 yd (452 m) per 3.5 oz (100 g)

Small amount of dark gray metallic crochet yarn

1 oz/30 g polyester toy filling

Cream sewing thread

Six black bugle beads

A small gold bead

Four small black buttons

A small piece of stiff gray or silver card stock

A piece of Velcro tape in white, measuring 1 x ³⁄₈ in (2.5 x 1 cm)

A piece of Velcro tape in white, measuring 2 x ³⁄₄ in (5 x 2 cm)

Two ¹⁄₂-in (13-mm) snap fasteners

YOU WILL ALSO NEED

A pair of U.S. 2/3 (3 mm) knitting needles

A pair of U.S. 2 (2.75 mm) knitting needles

Stitch holder or extra needle

A yarn needle to sew your items together

An embroidery needle

An ordinary sewing needle

A green crayon

THE DOLL

HEAD
MAKE 2 PIECES
- Using U.S. 2/3 (3 mm) needles, cast on 10 sts in light gray.
- 1st row: Inc1, K7, inc1, K1. (12 sts)
- Next row: P.
- Next row: K2, M1, K8, M1, K2. (14 sts)
- Work 17 rows in st st, beg with a P row.
- Next row: K2, k2tog, K6, ssk, K2. (12 sts)
- Next row: P2tog, P8, p2tog. (10 sts)
- Bind off.

INNER FACE
MAKE 1 PIECE
- Using U.S. 2/3 (3 mm) needles, cast on 10 sts in red.
- 1st row: Inc1, K7, inc1, K1. (12 sts)
- Next row: P.
- Next row: K2, M1, K8, M1, K2. (14 sts)
- Work 17 rows in st st, beg with a P row.
- Next row: K2, k2tog, K6, ssk, K2. (12 sts)
- Next row: P2tog, P8, p2tog. (10 sts)
- Bind off.

EARS
MAKE 2
- Using U.S. 2/3 (3 mm) needles, cast on 5 sts in light gray.
- 1st row: K.
- Next row: P2tog, K1, p2tog. (3 sts)
- Next row: S1, k2tog, psso.
- Break yarn and pull it through rem st.

UPPER BODY
The upper body is knitted from the top to the bottom.

FRONT
MAKE 1
- Using U.S. 2/3 (3 mm) needles, cast on 14 sts in light gray.
- Work 6 rows in st st, beg with a K row.
- Next row: Cast on 4 sts, K to end. (18 sts)
- Next row: Cast on 4 sts, P to end. (22 sts)
- Work 23 rows in st st, beg with a K row.
- Next row: P4, K14, P4.
- Next row: Bind off 4 sts, K to last 4 sts, bind off 4 sts. (14 sts)
- Break yarn and rejoin it to WS of work.
- Work 5 rows in st st, beg with a P row.
- Bind off.

BACK
MAKE 1
- Using U.S. 2/3 (3 mm) needles, cast on 14 sts in light gray.
- Work 24 rows in st st, beg with a K row.
- Bind off.

LOWER BODY
FRONT
MAKE 1
- Using U.S. 2/3 (3 mm) needles, cast on 14 sts in light gray.
- Work 6 rows in st st, beg with a K row.
- Next row: Cast on 4 sts, K to end. (18 sts)
- Next row: Cast on 4 sts, P to end. (22 sts)
- Work 7 rows in st st, beg with a K row.
- Next row: P4, K14, P4.
- Next row: Bind off 4 sts, K to last 4 sts, bind off 4 sts. (14 sts)
- Break yarn and rejoin it to WS of work.
- Work 5 rows in st st, beg with a P row.
- Bind off.

BACK
MAKE 1
- Using U.S. 2/3 (3 mm) needles, cast on 14 sts in light gray.
- Work 8 rows in st st, beg with a K row.
- Bind off.

FIRST LEG
MAKE 1
- Using U.S. 2/3 (3 mm) needles, cast on 30 sts in light gray.
- Work 6 rows in st st, beg with a K row.
- Next row: K6, bind off 18 sts, K to end. (12 sts) *
- Work 3 rows in st st, beg with a P row.
- Next row: K4, then turn and work on only these 4 sts, leaving rem 8 sts on needle.
- Work 6 rows in st st, beg with a P row.
- Break yarn and rejoin it to rem 8 sts on RS of work.
- Work 7 rows in st st, beg with a K row.
- Now work over all 12 sts.
- Work 13 rows in st st, beg with a P row.
- Bind off.

SECOND LEG
MAKE 1
- Work as for first leg until *.
- Work 23 rows in st st, beg with a P row.
- Bind off.

BONE
MAKE 1
- Using size U.S. 2 (2.75 mm) needles, cast on 7 sts in white.
- Work 12 rows in st st, beg with a K row.
- Bind off.

ARMS
MAKE 2
- Using U.S. 2/3 (3 mm) needles, cast on 4 sts in light gray.
- Work 4 rows in st st, beg with a K row.
- Next row: Cast on 3 sts, K to end. (7 sts)
- Next row: Cast on 3 sts, P to end. (10 sts)
- Work 28 rows in st st, beg with a K row.
- Next row: K1, k2tog, K4, ssk, K1. (8 sts)
- Next row: P2tog, P4, p2tog. (6 sts)
- Break yarn, thread it through rem sts, and secure.

MAKING UP AND DECORATING
Sew the body, arms, and legs together as outlined in the instructions on page 17.

Fold the bone in half lengthwise, so that the right side is on the outside. Whipstitch one of the short seams and the long seam. Stuff lightly and whipstitch the second short seam. Work a couple of stitches in the center of the short seam to make the bone end. Insert the bone into the gap in the leg. Overstitch it in light gray and work a few straight stitches across the bone where it meets the knitted flesh. Using a separated strand of red yarn, make a row of chain stitch down the side and underneath the protruding bone for the wound. Using a separated strand of black yarn, work a few straight stitches over the wound. Sew the black bugle beads in place on the arms for the fingernails.

For the head, place the two main head pieces right sides together. Place the red inner head piece face down on top of the two head pieces. Whipstitch around the edges of the head, using gray yarn and leaving a gap at one side of the head for turning and stuffing. Turn the head right side out. Because the head is made from three layers instead of two, you will have two "pockets." Make sure you stuff the section made up of the back of the head and the red inner part, so that the right side of the red inner part is facing toward the outside. Using red yarn, whipstitch the gap closed, so that the stuffing is held in but the side section of the front of the face is free to curl back. Using a separated strand of black yarn, make three straight stitches over the curled back edge of the face. Complete the head as outlined in the main instructions.

Whipstitch the ears in place.

Using black yarn, make two French knots for the eyes. Work an oval of chain stitches around the French knots, using white yarn. Make a few straight stitches in black mohair yarn for the eyebrows. Work the nose in chain stitch, using light gray yarn. Make a few French knots in light gray yarn on one of the cheeks. Work the outline of the mouth in chain stitch, using a separated strand of bright pink yarn. Work the center of the mouth in satin stitch, using black yarn and keeping your stitches vertical. Work a couple of straight stitches for the teeth, using pale green yarn. Make the mustache in chain stitch, using a separated strand of dark gray yarn. Sew the gold bead in place for the earring.

Shade in under the eyes, using the green crayon.

JACKET
MAKE 1

- Using U.S. 2/3 (3 mm) needles, cast on 42 sts in white.
- K 2 rows.
- Next row: K2, P38, K2.
- Next row: K.
- Rep last 2 rows 9 more times.
- Next row: K2, P38, K2.
- Next row: K13, then turn and work on only these sts, leaving rem sts on needle.
- Next row: P11, K2.
- Next row: K.
- Rep last 2 rows 2 more times.
- Break yarn and leave sts on needle.
- Rejoin yarn to rem sts on RS of work.
- Next row: K16, then turn and work on only these 16 sts.
- Work 6 rows in st st, beg with a P row.
- Break yarn and leave sts on needle.
- Rejoin yarn to rem 13 sts on RS of work.
- Next row: K.
- Next row: K2, P11.
- Next row: K.

- Rep last 2 rows 2 more times.
- Now work across all 42 st sts on needle.
- Next row: Bind off 7 sts pwise, K5 (6 sts on needle incl st rem from binding off), [k2tog] 3 times, K4, [ssk] 3 times, K13. (29 sts)
- Next row: Bind off 7 sts, K to end. (22 sts)
- Next row: K.
- Next row: K2tog, K18, ssk. (20 sts)
- Bind off.

SLEEVES
MAKE 2

- Using U.S. 2/3 (3 mm) needles, cast on 14 sts in white.
- 1st row: K.
- Work 24 rows in st st, beg with a K row.
- Bind off.

MAKING UP
With the right sides of the jacket together, whipstitch the shoulder seams. Sew the sleeve seams, using mattress stitch. Insert the sleeves into the armholes of the main piece and whipstitch them from the inside. Then overlap the right side of the jacket with the left. Sew on three of the buttons and sew the fourth button, leaving a longer length of thread so that it looks as if the button is falling off. Using red yarn, make a combination of French knots, some with straight stitches coming out in a star pattern, to represent splattered blood.

TOQUE HAT
MAKE 1

- Using U.S. 2/3 (3 mm) needles, cast on 30 sts in white.
- K 5 rows.
- Next row: K1, [inc1, K1] to last st, K1. (44 sts)
- Work 13 rows in st st, beg with a P row.
- Next row: [P2tog] 22 times. (22 sts)
- Next row: [K2tog] 11 times. (11 sts)
- Break yarn and thread through rem sts.

MAKING UP

Pull the yarn up somewhat firmly and sew the seam, using mattress stitch. Distress both the toque hat and the jacket, using a solution of black tea as described on page 78.

PANTS

The pants are knitted in two colors—navy and cream 4-ply yarn.

MAKE 1

- Using U.S. 2/3 (3 mm) needles, cast on 22 sts in navy 4-ply yarn for first leg.
- 1st row: [K1 navy, K1 cream] 11 times.
- Next row: [P1 cream, P1 navy] 11 times.
- Rep last 2 rows 9 more times and leave sts on stitch holder or extra needle.
- Cast on 22 sts in navy 4-ply yarn for second leg.
- 1st row: [K1 navy, K1 cream] 11 times.
- Next row: [P1 cream, P1 navy] 11 times.
- Rep last 2 rows 4 more times.
- Now work across all 40 sts.
- Work 14 rows in st st, beg with a K row, keeping to the navy/cream pattern.
- Break cream and cont in only navy yarn.
- K 4 rows.
- Bind off.

MAKING UP

Using mattress stitch, sew the back seam of the pants so that the lowest part of the seam is level with the crotch. Then sew the two inside leg seams, again using mattress stitch.

CLEAVER

MAKE 1

- Using U.S. 2 (2.75 mm) needles, cast on 14 sts in dark gray metallic crochet yarn.
- Work 11 rows in st st, beg with a K row.
- Next row: Bind off 4 sts, K5 (6 sts on needles incl st rem from binding off), bind off 4 sts. (6 sts)
- Break yarn and join dark brown yarn to RS of work.
- K 2 rows.
- Work 9 rows in st st, beg with a K row.
- Next row: K.
- Bind off.

MAKING UP

Cut a piece of card stock, using the template above on the left. Fold the cleaver piece in half lengthwise, with the right side facing outward, and whipstitch it around the card-stock template.

KNIFE

MAKE 1

- Using U.S. 2 (2.75 mm) needles, cast on 6 sts in dark brown.
- 1st row: K.
- Work 11 rows in st st, beg with a K row.
- Next row: K.
- Break yarn and join dark gray metallic crochet yarn to RS of work.
- Work 12 rows in st st, beg with a K row.
- Next row: K2 tog, K2, ssk. (4 sts)
- Next row: [P2tog] twice. (2 sts)
- Break yarn and thread it through rem sts.

MAKING UP

Cut a piece of card stock, using the template above on the right. Fold the knife piece in half lengthwise, with the right side facing outward, and whipstitch it around the card-stock template.

Biker Chick ZoMbIE

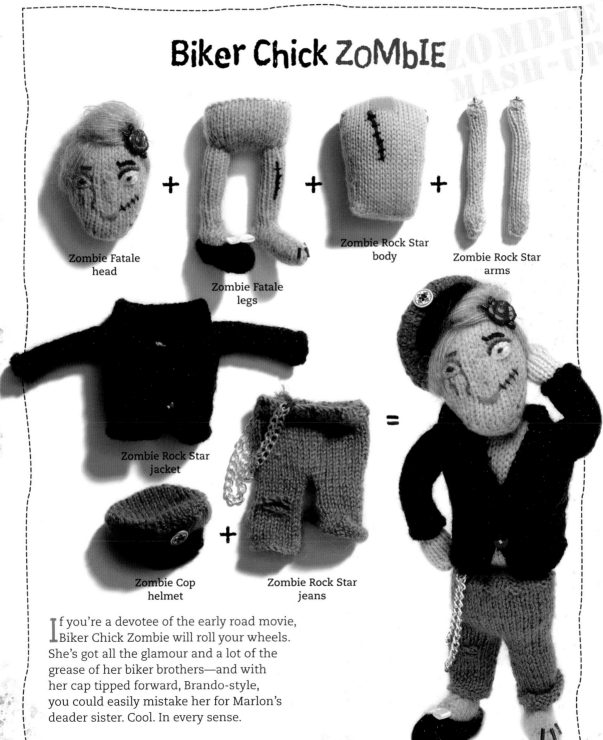

Zombie Fatale
head

+

Zombie Fatale
legs

+

Zombie Rock Star
body

+

Zombie Rock Star
arms

Zombie Rock Star
jacket

Zombie Cop
helmet

+

Zombie Rock Star
jeans

=

If you're a devotee of the early road movie, Biker Chick Zombie will roll your wheels. She's got all the glamour and a lot of the grease of her biker brothers—and with her cap tipped forward, Brando-style, you could easily mistake her for Marlon's deader sister. Cool. In every sense.

zombie GRaVE DIGGER

Being a zombie is an equal-opportunities business—there's no reason why grave digging should be left to the guys. Although this lady is in an advanced state of putrefaction, she's hanging onto her flowerpot hat. And she's in a growing business; you know that part in the horror movie when the graves all start heaving with their freshly dead occupants? It's a job to free them up to do their gruesome work—and that's why she needs the shovel.

PEDIGREE

1786 Ghouls—creatures found in Eastern myth, who live on newly dead human flesh and frequent graveyards—get their first mention in the novel *Vathek*, by author Samuel Beckford.

ca. 1900 The *calavera* (skeleton) prints (right) of the Mexican artist José Posada show skeletons engaged in everyday activities—and gain international popularity.

2011 Fantasy fiction moves right up to date with the publication of the fantasy/crime series, *iZombie*, featuring a detective who is also a (female) grave-digging zombie.

Zombie GraVE DiGgER

With a rope and shovel, the zombie grave digger specializes at freeing the undead. It's a dirty job, but somebody's got to do it! The drab colors and green, maggoty eye may not be immediately enchanting, but she still enjoys her accessories—her hat is decorated with the once-beautiful flowers from some poor soul's grave.

YOU WiLL NEED

1 skein dark gray DK yarn; 225 yd (206 m) per 3.5 oz (100 g)

Very small amount of pale green DK yarn

1 skein cream DK yarn; 225 yd (206 m) per 3.5 oz (100 g)

1 skein lilac DK yarn; 225 yd (206 m) per 3.5 oz (100 g)

Small amounts of mid-pink, flecked light brown, and teal DK yarns

Small amount of dark metallic silver crochet yarn

1 oz/30 g polyester toy filling

Cream sewing thread

One glass bead for the eye

Three 1/8-in (3-mm) white glass teardrop beads

A flower spray with wired stem

A small piece of stiff gray or silver card stock

A plastic drinking straw

Adhesive tape

A piece of Velcro tape in black measuring 1 x 3/8 in (2.5 x 1 cm)

A piece of Velcro tape in black measuring 2 x 3/4 in (5 x 2 cm)

Two 1/2-in (13-mm) snap fasteners

YOU WILL ALSO NEED

A pair of U.S. 2/3 (3 mm) knitting needles

A pair of U.S. 2 (2.75 mm) knitting needles

A size U.S. D-3 (3.25 mm) or similar size crochet hook

A yarn needle to sew your items together

An embroidery needle

An ordinary sewing needle

THE DOLL

HEAD
MAKE 2 PIECES
- Using U.S. 2/3 (3 mm) needles, cast on 10 sts in dark gray.
- Work 8 rows in st st, beg with a K row.
- Next row: K2, M1, K to last 2 sts, M1, K2. (12 sts)
- Next row: P.
- Rep last 2 rows 2 more times. (16 sts)
- Work 10 rows in st st, beg with a K row.
- Next row: K2, k2tog, K8, ssk, K2. (14 sts)
- Next row: P2tog, P10, p2tog. (12 sts)
- Bind off.

UPPER BODY
The upper body is knitted from the top to the bottom.

FRONT
MAKE 1
- Using U.S. 2/3 (3 mm) needles, cast on 14 sts in dark gray.
- Work 6 rows in st st, beg with a K row.
- Next row: Cast on 4 sts, K to end. (18 sts)
- Next row: Cast on 4 sts, P to end. (22 sts)
- Work 23 rows in st st, beg with a K row.
- Next row: P4, K14, P4.
- Next row: Bind off 4 sts, K to last 4 sts, bind off 4 sts. (14 sts)
- Break yarn and rejoin it to WS of work.
- Work 5 rows in st st, beg with a P row.
- Bind off.

BACK
MAKE 1
- Using U.S. 2/3 (3 mm) needles, cast on 14 sts in dark gray.

- Work 24 rows in st st, beg with a K row.
- Bind off.

LOWER BODY
FRONT
MAKE 1
- Using U.S. 2/3 (3 mm) needles, cast on 14 sts in dark gray.
- Work 6 rows in st st, beg with a K row.
- Next row: Cast on 4 sts, K to end. (18 sts)
- Next row: Cast on 4 sts, P to end. (22 sts)
- Work 7 rows in st st, beg with a K row.
- Next row: P4, K14, P4.
- Next row: Bind off 4 sts, K to last 4 sts, bind off 4 sts. (14 sts)
- Break yarn and rejoin it to WS of work.
- Work 5 rows in st st, beg with a P row.
- Bind off.

BACK
MAKE 1
- Using U.S. 2/3 (3 mm) needles, cast on 14 sts in dark gray.
- Work 8 rows in st st, beg with a K row.
- Bind off.

LEGS
MAKE 2
- Using U.S. 2/3 (3 mm) needles, cast on 30 sts in dark gray.
- Work 6 rows in st st, beg with a K row.
- Next row: K6, bind off 18 sts, K to end. (12 sts)
- Work 23 rows in st st, beg with a P row.
- Bind off.

ARMS
MAKE 2
- Using U.S. 2/3 (3 mm) needles, cast on 4 sts in dark gray.
- Work 4 rows in st st, beg with a K row.
- Next row: Cast on 3 sts, K to end. (7 sts)
- Next row: Cast on 3 sts, P to end. (10 sts)
- Work 28 rows in st st, beg with a K row.
- Next row: K1, k2tog, K4, ssk, K1. (8 sts)
- Next row: P2tog, P4, p2tog. (6 sts)
- Break yarn, thread it through rem sts, and secure.

MAGGOTS
MAKE 3
Using the crochet hook, work a ³⁄₈-inch (1-cm) crochet chain for each maggot, using pale green yarn.

MAKING UP AND DECORATING
Sew the head, body, arms, and legs together as outlined in the instructions on page 17.

Using cream yarn, embroider the bones, ribs, and skull in chain stitch, using both the main photo and the body parts close-ups (above) to guide you. The kneecaps are formed from a small circle of chain stitches. Add straight stitches to the spine to represent the vertebrae and across the beginning of the foot.

Make one eye socket in chain stitch, using cream yarn. Thread the yarn tail at one end of each maggot up through the crochet chain and pull slightly to make the maggot curl. Use the yarn tails to secure the maggots to the eye socket. Attach the glass bead for the second eye and make a few rows of chain stitch around the eye, using cream yarn. Work three straight stitches in cream yarn to form a triangle for the nose. Work a straight stitch in cream yarn for the mouth and attach the three white teardrop beads for the teeth.

HAT
SIDE AND RIM
MAKE 1
- Using U.S. 2/3 (3 mm) needles, cast on 35 sts in lilac.
- Work 14 rows in st st, beg with a K row.
- Bind off.
- With RS facing, pick up and knit 35 sts along cast-on edge.
- Next row: P.
- Next row: K1, [inc1] 33 times, K1. (68 sts)
- Work 2 rows in st st, beg with a P row.
- Bind off kwise.

TIP
MAKE 1
- Using U.S. 2/3 (3 mm) needles, cast on 7 sts in lilac.
- 1st row: Inc1, K4, inc1, K1. (9 sts)
- Next row: P.
- Next row: K1, M1, K to last st, M1, K1. (11 sts)
- Next row: P.

- Rep last 2 rows 2 more times. (15 sts)
- Next row: K1, k2tog, K to last 3 sts, ssk, K1. (13 sts)
- Next row: P.
- Rep last 2 rows 2 more times. (9 sts)
- Next row: K1, k2tog, K3, ssk, K1. (7 sts)
- Bind off pwise.

MAKING UP
Sew the back seam of the side and rim of the hat, using mattress stitch. Whipstitch the tip of the hat to the sides, working from the inside. Wrap the mid-pink yarn around the hat to represent the hatband and secure. Wrap the wired stem of the flower around the yarn hatband.

ROPE
MAKE 1
- Using the crochet hook, make a 2-foot (60-cm) crochet chain, using flecked light brown yarn.

SHOVEL
BLADE
MAKE 2 PIECES
- Using U.S. 2 (2.75 mm) needles, cast on 14 sts in metallic silver crochet yarn.
- Work 10 rows in st st, beg with a K row.
- Next row: K1, k2tog, K8, ssk, k1. (12 sts)
- Next row: P.
- Next row: K1, k2tog, K6, ssk, K1. (10 sts)
- Next row: P2tog, P6, p2tog. (8 sts)
- Next row: K1, k2tog, K2, ssk, K1. (6 sts)
- Next row: P2tog, K2, p2tog. (4 sts)
- Next row: [K2tog] twice. (2 sts)
- Next row: P2tog.
- Break yarn and pull through rem st.

HANDLE
MAKE 1
- Using U.S. 2 (2.75 mm) needles, cast on 28 sts in teal.
- Work 3 rows in st st, beg with a K row.
- Bind off kwise.

MAKING UP
Place the two blade pieces together, with the right sides facing outward. Whipstitch the two sides, leaving the top edge open. Cut a piece of card stock, using the template shown to the right. Cut the drinking straw into a 4-inch (10-cm) length. Trim the last ³/₈ inch (1 cm) of the end of the drinking straw into a V-shape point and make two ³/₈-inch (1-cm) slits from the sides of the point. Place the card-stock blade between the pointed ends of the straw and secure with adhesive tape. Insert the card stock into the knitted blade and sew the top edges up to the sides of the handle. Wrap the knitted handle around the straw, so that the reverse of the stockinette stitch is on the outside, and whipstitch the long seam, starting from the top end. Secure the handle to the top of the blade with teal yarn and work a long V shape on each side of the blade, using chain stitch. Fill in with a few straight stitches.

Zombie Rock Star

Flamboyant hair, plenty of chains, and a broad, toothy smile—too bad his brains were half fried even before the zombie plague caught him. Still, if they get uncomfortable, they're only loosely attached to the rest of him. Even if he's undead, the star in him is determined to play on—there are still fans to satisfy. And if you don't want to knit a rock star, he can easily be converted to the undead leader of a biker gang: Just embroider a skull-and-crossbones on the back of his jacket.

Pedigree

1985 Inspired by the 1932 movie, the musician and movie director Rob Zombie names his heavy metal band White Zombie (right).

2000 *Wild Zero*, surely one of the oddest cult movies ever—a combination of Japanese garage rock, aliens, and zombies—wins several awards in the horror/comedy categories on the independent circuit.

2005 Renee Cooper launches her act, Zombie Girl. No reason for all zombie rockers to be male.

zombie RoCK STaR

This stomping zombie has toned down his fast-paced lifestyle just a little since he left the land of the living. The very best thing about him is that you can arrange his hair in a variety of attractive styles—try out a Mohawk by taking out his brain and tucking most of the hair, except for the ends, inside the brain pouch. And there are plenty of other possibilities . . .

YOU WILL NEED

1 skein light beige DK yarn; 225 yd (206 m) per 3.5 oz (100 g)

Small amounts of pale pink, red, mid-pink, green, fuzzy light brown, and cream DK yarns

Very small amounts of black and white DK yarns

1 skein sparkly black DK yarn; 225 yd (206 m) per 3.5 oz (100 g)

1 skein denim blue DK yarn; 225 yd (206 m) per 3.5 oz (100 g)

1 skein dark brown DK yarn; 225 yd (206 m) per 3.5 oz (100 g)

Cream sewing thread

1 oz/30 g polyester toy filling

A silver skull charm

A metal snake charm

A 9½-in (24-cm) length of waxed black cord

A small blue button

A 10¼-in (26-cm) length of silver metal chain

A piece of Velcro tape in beige, measuring 1 x ³⁄₈ in (2.5 x 1 cm)

A piece of Velcro tape in beige, measuring 2 x ¾ in (5 x 2 cm)

Two ½-in (13-mm) snap fasteners

YOU WILL ALSO NEED

A pair of U.S. 2/3 (3 mm) knitting needles

A pair of U.S. 2 (2.75 mm) knitting needles

A yarn needle to sew your items together

An embroidery needle

An ordinary sewing needle

A gray crayon

THE DOLL
HEAD
MAKE 2 PIECES
- Using U.S. 2/3 (3 mm) needles, cast on 18 sts in pale green.
- 1st row: Inc1, K15, inc1, K1. (20 sts)
- Work 3 rows in st st, beg with a P row.
- Next row: K2, k2tog, K to last 4 sts, ssk, K2. (18 sts)
- Work 3 rows in st st, beg with a P row.
- Rep last 4 rows 1 more time. (16 sts)
- Work 10 rows in st st, beg with a K row.
- Next row: K2, k2tog, K8, ssk, K2. (14 sts)
- Next row: P2tog, P10, p2tog. (12 sts)
- Bind off.

BRAIN POCKET
MAKE 1
- Using U.S. 2/3 (3 mm) needles, cast on 12 sts in light beige.
- Work 4 rows in st st, beg with a K row.
- Next row: K2, M1, K8, M1, K2. (14 sts)
- Work 13 rows in st st, beg with a P row.
- Next row: K2, k2tog, K to last 4 sts, ssk, K2. (12 sts)
- Work 3 rows in st st, beg with a P row.
- Bind off.

BRAIN
MAKE 2 PIECES
- Using size U.S. 2 (2.75 mm) needles, cast on 5 sts in pink.
- 1st row: Inc1, K to last 2 sts, inc1, K1. (7 sts)
- Next row: P.
- Rep last 2 rows 2 more times. (11 sts)

- Work 4 rows in st st, beg with a K row.
- Next row: K1, k2tog, K to last 3 sts, ssk, K1. (9 sts)
- Next row: P.
- Rep last 2 rows 1 more time. (7 sts)
- Next row: K1, k2tog, K1, ssk, K1. (5 sts)
- Bind off kwise.

UPPER BODY
The upper body is knitted from the top to the bottom.
FRONT
MAKE 1
- Using U.S. 2/3 (3 mm) needles, cast on 20 sts in light beige.
- Work 6 rows in st st, beg with a K row.
- Next row: Cast on 4 sts, K to end. (24 sts)
- Next row: Cast on 4 sts, P to end. (28 sts)
- Work 6 rows in st st, beg with a K row.
- Next row: K4, k2tog, K to last 6 sts, ssk, K4. (26 sts)
- Work 5 rows in st st, beg with a P row.
- Rep last 6 rows 2 more times. (22 sts)
- Next row: K.
- Next row: P4, K14, P4.
- Next row: Bind off 4 sts, K to last 4 sts, bind off 4 sts. (14 sts)
- Break yarn and rejoin it to WS of work.
- Work 5 rows in st st, beg with a P row.
- Bind off.

BACK
MAKE 1
- Using U.S. 2/3 (3 mm) needles, cast on 20 sts in light beige.
- Work 4 rows in st st, beg with a K row.

- Next row: K2, k2tog, K to last 4 sts, ssk, K2. (18 sts)
- Work 5 rows in st st, beg with a P row.
- Rep last 6 rows 2 more times. (14 sts)
- Bind off.

LOWER BODY
FRONT
MAKE 1
- Using U.S. 2/3 (3 mm) needles, cast on 14 sts in light beige.
- Work 6 rows in st st, beg with a K row.
- Next row: Cast on 4 sts, K to end. (18 sts)
- Next row: Cast on 4 sts, P to end. (22 sts)
- Work 7 rows in st st, beg with a K row.
- Next row: P4, K14, P4.
- Next row: Bind off 4 sts, K to last 4 sts, bind off 4 sts. (14 sts)

- Break yarn and rejoin it to WS of work.
- Work 5 rows in st st, beg with a P row.
- Bind off.

BACK
MAKE 1
- Using U.S. 2/3 (3 mm) needles, cast on 14 sts in light beige.
- Work 8 rows in st st, beg with a K row.
- Bind off.

LEGS
MAKE 2
- Using U.S. 2/3 (3 mm) needles, cast on 28 sts in light beige.
- Work 6 rows in st st, beg with a K row.
- Next row: K6, bind off 16 sts, K to end. (12 sts)
- Work 21 rows in st st, beg with a P row.
- Bind off.

ARMS
MAKE 2
- Using U.S. 2/3 (3 mm) needles,

cast on 4 sts in light beige.
- Work 4 rows in st st, beg with a K row.
- Next row: Cast on 3 sts, K to end. (7 sts)
- Next row: Cast on 3 sts, P to end. (10 sts)
- Work 24 rows in st st, beg with a K row.
- Next row: K2, M1, K3, M1, K3, M1, K2. (13 sts)
- Work 3 rows in st st, beg with a P row.
- Next row: K2, k2tog, K5, ssk, K2. (11 sts)
- Next row: P2tog, P7, p2tog. (9 sts)
- Bind off.

MAKING UP AND DECORATING
Sew the body, arms, and legs together as outlined in the instructions on page 17.

Use a separated strand of red yarn to work a row of chain stitch down the chest to make a "wound." Use a separated

strand of black yarn to make a series of short straight stitches across the wound.

Sew the head together as outlined in the general instructions on page 17, but stuff fairly lightly and do not close the top of the head at this stage. Fold the brain pocket lengthwise, so that the right sides are together, and whipstitch the seams. Insert the pocket into the top of the head so that the seams are at the sides and the right side of the knitting is on the inside of the pocket. Whipstitch the pocket to the top of the head around the edges.

Place the two brain pieces right sides together and whipstitch around the edges, leaving a gap for turning and stuffing. Turn the brain right side out, stuff it, and close the gap. Using mid-pink yarn, work a row of chain stitch up the center of the piece on both sides. Using mid-pink yarn, work a coiling shape of chain stitch along each half of the shape on both sides of the piece.

Before sewing the features on the face, make sure the brain pocket is pulled out. Using black yarn, sew two French knots for the eyes. Make a semicircle of chain stitches in white yarn under one French knot and in red yarn under the other. Work a straight stitch in black yarn across the top of each eye. Using mid-pink yarn, make five French knots on one cheek, wrapping the yarn just once around the needle instead of twice. Work the nose in chain stitch, using light beige yarn. Using black yarn, work the outline of the mouth in chain stitch and the center of the mouth in satin stitch, keeping the stitches vertical. Using a separated strand of red yarn, work around one side of the mouth in chain stitch. Make two straight stitches in white and three straight stitches in green for the teeth.

Shade in the eye sockets, using the gray crayon.

For the hair, cut eighteen 8-inch (20-cm) lengths of fuzzy light brown yarn and six 8-inch (20-cm) lengths of green yarn. Arrange them into six bunches, each with three lengths of brown and one length of green yarn. Space the bunches evenly around the rim of the head, securing them at the center of the bunches.

Tie the skull and snake pendant charms onto the black waxed cord and then tie it around the doll's neck.

JACKET
MAKE 1
- Using U.S. 2/3 (3 mm) needles, cast on 42 sts in sparkly black.
- K 2 rows.
- Next and every WS row: K2, P to last 2 sts, K2.
- Next RS row: K.

- Next RS row: K12, M1, K1, M1, K16, M1, K1, M1, K12. (46 sts)
- Next RS row: K.
- Next RS row: K.
- Next RS row: K13, M1, K1, M1, K18, M1, K1, M1, K13. (50 sts)
- Next RS row: K.
- Next RS row: K.
- Next RS row: K14, M1, K1, M1, K20, M1, K1, M1, K14. (54 sts)
- Next RS row: K.
- Next RS row: K.
- Next RS row: K16, then turn and work on only these 16 sts, leaving rem sts on needle.
- Next row: P14, K2.
- Next row: K.
- Rep last 2 rows 2 more times.
- Break yarn and rejoin it to sts rem on needle on RS of work.
- Next row: K22, then turn and work on only these 22 sts, leaving rem sts on needle.
- Work 6 rows in st st, beg with a P row.
- Break yarn and rejoin it to 16 sts rem on needle on RS of work.
- Next row: K.

- Next row: K2, P14.
- Next row: K.
- Rep these 2 rows 2 more times.
- Now work across all 54 sts.
- Next row: Bind off 3 sts, K12 (13 sts on needle incl st left from binding off), [k2tog] 4 times, K6, [ssk] 4 times, K to end. (43 sts)
- Next row: Bind off 3 sts, K to end. (40 sts)
- K 7 rows.
- Bind off.

SLEEVES
MAKE 2
- Using U.S. 2/3 (3 mm) needles, cast on 14 sts in sparkly black.
- 1st row: K.
- Work 22 rows in st st, beg with a K row.
- Bind off.

MAKING UP
With the right sides of the jacket together, whipstitch the shoulder seams. Sew the sleeve seams, using mattress stitch, then insert the sleeves into the jacket armholes and whipstitch them from the inside. On the reverse of the jacket, embroider a simple skull, using cream yarn. Work the outside in chain stitch. Make two French knots for the eyes and work straight stitches for the nose and mouth. Overlap the left border over the right border and sew on the small blue button.

PANTS
MAKE 1
- Using U.S. 2/3 (3 mm) needles, cast on 20 sts in denim blue 4-ply for first leg.
- Work 10 rows in st st, beg with a K row.
- Next row: K3, bind off 4 sts, K to end.
    - Next row: P13, turn work and cast on 4 sts, turn back again and P to end.
- Work 6 rows in st st, beg with a K row.
- Break yarn and leave sts on needle.
- Cast on 20 sts for second leg.
    - Work 18 rows in st st, beg with a K row.

- Next row: K 20 sts from second leg, then 20 sts from first leg. (40 sts)
- Work 15 rows in st st, beg with a P row.
- Next row: [K2, P2] to end.
- Rep last row 3 more times.
- Bind off, keeping to the K2, P2 pattern.

MAKING UP
Using mattress stitch, sew the back seam of the pants so that the lowest part of the seam is level with the crotch. Sew the inside leg seam of the first leg, again using mattress stitch. Sew the top 4 rows of the second leg seam. Sew the chain to the waistband of the pants.

BOOTS
MAKE 2
- Using U.S. 2/3 (3 mm) needles, cast on 30 sts in dark brown.
- K 2 rows.
- Work 4 rows in st st, beg with a K row.
- Next row: K8, bind off 14 sts, K to end. (16 sts)
- Work 7 rows in st st, beg with a P row.
- Next row: P.
- Bind off pwise.

MAKING UP
Fold the pieces widthwise, so that the right sides are together. Whipstitch the back, lower, and upper seams, then turn the boots right side out. To make the hole in one of the boots, make a ring of chain stitch around the end of the boot. Trim away the knitting on the toe end of the boot and fray the edges a little.

Yoga ZOMbIE

Zombie Grave
Digger head

Zombie Grave
Digger legs

Zombie Grave
Digger arms

Zombie Grave
Digger body

The Mummy grave
bandage

Zombie Cop
truncheon

It's a gift to be simple—and there's nothing much simpler than Yoga Zombie. Easing his rattling bones into the full lotus position, he stares serenely ahead, although maggots writhe on his cheek. His turban is easily achieved with just a yard of grave bandage (see page 78) and a couple of pins to keep it in place, topped off by a femur he found lying around (experienced knitters may recognize Zombie Cop's truncheon). Ommmmm.

The MuMMY

All the zombies in this book are suitable for the mummified stained bandage treatment—so you can easily create two different zombie looks from one zombie knit.

PEDiGrEE

1850 "Some Words with A Mummy," a short story by Edgar Allan Poe, offers a wry dialogue with a very sophisticated and eloquent Egyptian mummy.

1922 Howard Carter's discovery of the tomb of Tutankhamen, complete with the king's mummified body, kicks off a popular craze for all things Egyptian. Mummies begin to star in pulp novels and the seeds are sewn for the mummy's future in Hollywood.

YOU WiLL NEED

1 skein white DK yarn; 225 yd (206 m) per 3.5 oz (100 g)

YOU WILL ALSO NEED

A pair of size 3 mm (US 2/3) knitting needles

Red food coloring

A recently used tea bag or some strong black tea

BANDAGE

- Cast on 6 sts in white.
- Beg with a K row, work in st st until strip measures 10 feet (3 m).
- Bind off.

MAKING UP

Sew in yarn ends. To give the bandage a bloodied, worn look, wipe on some undiluted red food coloring for the blood and splash on some strong black tea, or dab the bandage with a damp, used tea bag for the stains. The bandage is long enough to wrap the entire doll several times. Wrap it around a couple of times to secure it at your starting point and tuck in the end when you have finished.